South Africa

*Revolution
or
Reconciliation?*

The Institute on Religion & Democracy

South Africa

Revolution or Reconciliation?

Walter H. Kansteiner

BRISTOL BOOKS®

WILMORE, KY 40390

To My Wife, Franny

SOUTH AFRICA: REVOLUTION OR RECONCILIATION?
© 1990 by Walter Kansteiner
Published by Bristol Books in cooperation with the Institute on Religion and Democracy

Revised Edition, January 1990

This book was originally published in 1988 by the Institute on Religion and Democracy, 729 15th St., N.W., Suite 900, Washington, D.C. 20005 (202-393-3200).

NOTICE:
The author wrote this book while still on staff at the Institute on Religion and Democracy. The text in no way should be construed as official United States Government policy.

Library of Congress Card Number: 89-62524
ISBN: 0-917851-44-7

BRISTOL BOOKS
An imprint of The Forum for Scriptural Christianity, Inc.
308 East Main Street • Wilmore, KY 40390

Contents

Acknowledgments

This book has truly been a cooperative effort, and I would be remiss if I did not express at the outset my gratitude to the many who helped produce it. I am particularly indebted to the Earhart Foundation for awarding me a grant to conduct the necessary research. In extending the grant to me, the foundation exerted no control or supervision, directly or indirectly, over the book's contents or conclusions. I am also grateful to all of my colleagues at IRD who were always ready and generous with their time and assistance.

I want to thank Ambassador Herman Nickel, Pastor Richard John Neuhaus, Dr. Dean Curry, Dr. Kent Hill, Diane Knippers, Amy Sherman and Alan Wisdom for reviewing the manuscript and providing numerous suggestions. George Weigel was particularly helpful with the chapter on just-revolution theory. All opinions and errors, of course, remain the sole responsibility of the author.

A collective thank you is extended to the 50 or more South Africans of all political hues, from leaders of the ANC to the Conservative Party, who were willing to be interviewed. Through this process I have made friendships that I hope and trust will last a lifetime.

I am grateful to Randy Tift for a masterful job in coordinating much of the research and helping me with the initial drafts. Thanks also to Victoria Thomas who helped in the final manuscript preparation for the first edition, and to Dana Preusch who assisted with the second.

Finally I want to thank my wife, Frances, and my daughter, Beverly, for their never-ending patience and acceptance of my frequent traveling and long hours of writing.

Foreword

This is a book about South Africa today, and a subject that has a compelling claim upon all who care about political justice. But it is also a book about a question that is pertinent far beyond the borders of South Africa. That question has to do with how we think about revolution as an instrument of political, social and economic change.

Twenty years ago I wrote, with Peter Berger, *Movement and Revolution*. My part of that project was to explore the ways in which the criteria for a *justified war* might also apply to a justified revolution. It was unabashedly a moral reflection, recognizing that both the ends we choose and the means we choose to reach those ends depend upon judgments that are moral in nature. In the present work Walter Kansteiner has very ably extended that reflection to the particular case of South Africa.

Of course there are those who claim that, with respect to South Africa, choosing is a thing of the past. All the choices have been exhausted, it is said, and now the oppressed peoples of South Africa must face the fact that the revolutionary option is forced upon them. Human beings, if they are to be truly human, have a moral obligation to resist and, if necessary, to defy all such determinist formulas that would trample underfoot our responsibilities as moral agents. To be sure, part of the debate about South Africa is over different readings of reality or, as some prefer, different readings of the "signs of the times." But we must be aware of the sometimes elusive ways in which the cognitive is influenced by the volitional. To put it more simply, we all have a powerful tendency to see what we want to see.

In any situation of conflict, we should begin from a presumption against the use of violence and force. That underscores the importance of the "last resort" criterion in thinking about justified revolution. The argument is sometimes made that only the people most immediately involved have the right to make judgments about if and when revolution is justified. But I believe that argument is wrong-headed on at least two scores. First, if we give in to it, we are abdicating our own moral responsibility. Those who are involved in advocating policies with respect to South Africa have

8

an obligation to assume moral responsibility for the policies they advocate. It is not enough to say, for example, that we are simply standing in solidarity with the people of South Africa. That leads directly to the second problem with such an abdication, namely that we are responsible for deciding just who among the people of South Africa, or even the black people of South Africa, we are standing in solidarity with.

Kansteiner's study helps us to confront these questions honestly. This is not an exercise in the kind of complexifying that leads to inaction; it is not an instance of "analysis for paralysis." On the contrary, it leads us to the most active engagement in sorting through different analyses and different proposed courses of action to make whatever conclusions we reach truly our own. We must accept responsibility not only for the policies that we advocate, but also for the consequences of those policies. Some of us learned this the hard way in Vietnam. When we were cautioned about the "bloodbath" that would occur after U.S. withdrawal, a common response was to say that nobody could know what would happen, but "whatever happens, it could not be worse that what is happening now." Of course that response turned out to be dreadfully wrong. By the most elementary measures of human suffering—the body count of the dead and the rivers of blood—what happened in Indochina in the years following U.S. withdrawal in 1975 was much, much worse than the war that we so earnestly wanted to bring to an end.

Admittedly, this is grisly business, comparing body counts, trying to develop a comparative calculus of human misery. But it is a grisly business that cannot be avoided by those who do not want to be accused of playing with the lives of other people. If I may be so shameless as to refer again to my own work, two years ago I published *Dispensations: The Future of South Africa as South Africans See It.* I am often asked how I think that work stands up in the light of subsequent events. You might think I would be happy to report, but in fact I am very sorry to report, that it stands up very well indeed. In contrast to the simplistic picture conveyed by our media, and by some activists on the Left and the Right, the myriad of groups, tensions, interests and aspirations of the people of South Africa are maddeningly diverse. It is a strength of Walter Kansteiner's study that he recognizes that diversity and what it means for the alternative courses of action proposed, including the course of revolutionary warfare.

The present government of South Africa claims that it has abandoned apartheid in principle and is working hard to abandon it in practice. Critics of the government are understandably suspicious of that claim and some assert that the many "reforms" of recent years have only entrenched apartheid more deeply. Certainly South Africa is a long way from the full incorporation of its people into a democratic polity—that is putting it very gently indeed. The level of distrust and fear within South Africa, even among the black groups of South Africa, is difficult to overestimate. The hope, to many of us who watch South Africa, is in the development of institutions that can contain the consequences of distrust. That development is an arduous process and it may be, as many claim, that "time has run out." One should at least keep in mind, however, that with respect to South Africa, people have been saying for 50 years now that time has run out.

The end that must be pursued, I believe, is majority rule achieved with a minimum of bloodshed and suffering, resulting in a more democratic rather than less democratic regime, and maintaining the economic base of a country that is potentially prosperous for all. Walter Kansteiner does not know, I do not know and nobody knows whether that threefold end can be realized. What Walter Kansteiner offers here is an informed and informative exploration into possibilities that may preclude the worse from becoming the worst.

Richard John Neuhaus
Institute on Religion and Public Life
New York, New York

Preface to the Second Edition

The first edition of *South Africa: Revolution or Reconciliation* was written in early 1988, a time when South Africa was still catching its breath from the intense violence of the 1984-1986 period. The second edition was completed in June 1989 and discusses numerous developments—domestically, regionally and internationally—which have had direct repercussions inside South Africa.

Domestically a new attitude seems to be emerging from within the ranks of both white and black leadership. Perhaps this new approach can best be labeled "pragmatic." The resignation of P.W. Botha and a number of his cabinet ministers signals the beginning of a new administration, which carries with it a multitude of new hopes and visions. F.W. de Klerk's leadership will be critical in determining South Africa's next decade.

Regionally the Angolan-Namibian Peace settlement produces a vast array of new possibilities for southern Africa as a region and the Republic in particular. Internationally the U.S.-Soviet relationship and Moscow's approach toward southern Africa bodes well for positive development. All of these factors have been reflected in numerous changes and additions in almost every chapter of this second edition.

Introduction

For many in the West, South Africa is a nation in utter turmoil, a revolution waiting to happen. The image of South Africa that often rushes to mind is one of white army units in full riot gear snapping huge whips known as *sjamboks*. And young black youths fleeing through the dusty streets of Soweto as young white Afrikaners fire tear gas in every direction.

Or we are assailed by the particularly haunting image of a middle-aged black man running for his life from an angry black crowd, which eventually catches him, forces a kerosene-doused tire over his neck and sets him ablaze. The crime which earned him this awful punishment—"collaboration with the racist oppressor."

These images are rooted in real events and they could occur again. But when you step off the plane in the warm South African morning sunshine at Jan Smuts Airport, revolution is not the first thing that greets you. In fact, South Africa appears on the surface to be an ordered society with a respectable GNP growth rate, transportation and communication systems that work, and a certain degree of toleration within the multi-ethnic culture.

This apparent calm, however, is currently resting on a political foundation known as apartheid. The apartheid system affects every inhabitant of South Africa, regardless of race, education, or vocation. At birth each child must be registered by his parents in a racial category. That racial classification will determine where the child lives, where he goes to school and if he can vote. Such discrimination, enshrined in law and practice, breeds a discontent which undermines any hope for a stable, peaceful society.

South Africa has been a land of very little calm. Since the 17th century, when the Dutch first established Cape Town as a trading station, there has often been struggle between the many ethnic and racial groups that have called this home. The British settlements that were established along the coast during the 18th and 19th centuries brought conflict not only between white European settlers and black Africans, but also between the Dutch (Afrikaners) and the British.

The Afrikaners, who had left the coastal areas and made the "trek" inland to avoid living under the British, ended up sitting on the biggest prize yet—gold, diamonds and what would become "strategic minerals." The English, led by Cecil Rhodes and others, coveted the bounty of the Transvaal (the Afrikaner republic in the north) and the Boer War was on. As the Europeans fought over the treasures that lay under the African soil, black Africans were caught in an alien power struggle. The war ended with a British victory in 1902, but one of the war's legacies was a deep-seated animosity between the Afrikaner and English populations.

Until 1948 South Africa was governed by the English-speaking whites who focused their attention on commercial and industrial expansion. However, by the end of World War II the Afrikaners made up the majority of the white population and the National Party swept to power in 1948.

The National Party was a *volk* or people-oriented party whose primary objective was to look after the welfare of the Afrikaner. Highly nationalistic with very real tendencies toward a centrally-planned economy, the *Nats* built a government bureaucracy that provided thousands of jobs to their volk. In creating this preferential world, the National Party embraced the policy of "apartheid" or separate development. Blacks were restricted in where they could live, what jobs they could hold and who they could marry. Many of these apartheid laws have been scrapped in recent years, but the obstacles to black political power have remained.

In the past 30 years South Africa has experienced numerous cycles of violence. The pattern is usually one of serious township violence, followed by repression and then a state of relative calm. Like the pangs of childbirth, these cycles appear to be coming more often and with greater intensity. In 1985 and 1986 the Western world received a nightly television dosage of South Africa in turmoil. White soldiers were seen rolling through black townships in armored personnel carriers. Black policemen were pictured barely controlling fierce German shepherds set to attack black crowds. Rocks, sticks and tear gas canisters were constantly propelled into air already thick with black smoke from burning tires. Revolution looked like it was near at hand, if not in full swing.

Then on June 12, 1986, a State of Emergency was imposed. The lid was placed on top of the simmering pot. A calm returned to the townships. Schools were once again filled with students, some of whom had been out for nearly two years. Parents went

back to work. The relative stability is occasionally disrupted by
new government bannings and arrests, such as those which occurred in early 1988, but the notion of a full-blown revolution has
once again been pushed to a back burner.

While the surface calm has reappeared for now, the most
detrimental product of the cycle of violence, the polarization of
society, continues to widen. South Africa is increasingly emerging
as a nation with two distasteful extremes: authoritarianism on the
Right and potential totalitarianism on the Left. The white extremists, symbolized by the Afrikaner Resistance Movement
(AWB), call for a return to strict apartheid and greater political and
economic control vested in the central (Afrikaner-controlled)
government. One cannot help being reminded of the Nazi Party in
the early 1930s. Equally foreboding is the African National
Congress's (ANC) call for a violent revolution and for some within
the ANC, a vision of a one-party Marxist-oriented state.

Those who are truly committed to justice and freedom, both
inside and outside of South Africa, must reject both of these
alternatives, resist further polarization of South African society
and opt to support a third choice: a "democratic middle ground."
This third option is one that follows a path toward true democracy
in a nonracial, multiparty state with guarantees of individual liberties and freedoms.

As a people who have experienced racial tensions and found
some solutions, Americans find it terribly easy to scramble to the
moralistic "high road" and heap accusations and platitudes upon
all associated with South Africa. It is also tempting to try to
understand the South African dilemma narrowly within the dimensions of America's own civil rights movement. This book attempts
to avoid both of these traps and to assess the South African
situation within the framework of the Christian just-war tradition.

The first chapter briefly introduces the just-war tradition,
where it fits within Christian thinking on war and peace issues and
how it can be helpful in assessing a revolutionary situation. The
next five chapters look at how each of the *ad bellum criteria* apply
to South Africa in the late 1980s. The criteria —revolution due to
injury, revolution by a legitimate authority, revolution with right
intentions, revolution as a last resort and revolution with a
reasonable hope of success—will be analyzed and conclusions
drawn.

The second part of this work focuses on how South Africa can avoid the extremes and pursue a course towards a truly democratic nation. The choice between a neo-apartheid government or an armed revolution to install a one-party regime is no choice at all. The true democrats in South Africa, those who occupy the "middle ground," must be bolstered in their efforts to bring about authentic reform. Building a constitutional democracy in a post-apartheid South Africa will be a long, arduous task. There will be many on the Left who will characterize the democrats as acquiescing in the injustices of apartheid, and on the Right the reformers will be branded as communist stooges. Though these unfair critics pose a serious obstacle to progress, the democrats clearly possess a reasonable hope of success.

Chapter nine deals with a particularly troubling roadblock: the romantic revolutionaries. These "slide-away liberals" have abandoned their true liberal principles and adopted the more flashy rhetoric and simpler solutions of the armed revolution. The subsequent chapter examines why South Africa's middle-ground liberals have a good chance of succeeding. The economy, ongoing and future negotiations and efforts toward reconciliation can bring a final end to apartheid without armed revolution. The final chapters look at how Americans can assist in supporting the democrats in South Africa: what U.S. foreign policy should and should not include, and how the U.S. private sector (the churches, the corporations, the academe and the media) can throw their weight behind those attempting to build a new, democratic South Africa.

Any book on South Africa, particularly one that examines revolution in that country, cannot avoid the sometimes raw emotion that the subject conjures up. But to be swept away with the tumultuous rhetoric that frequently accompanies the topic helps little in understanding or improving the situation on the ground. This book is written particularly for those who seek some insight into the confusing and troubling world of South Africa. For only when compassion is wedded to understanding is there any hope for responsible action.

Part I

Revolution and South Africa

One

The Just-War Tradition

Hurrah for revolution and more cannon-shot!
A beggar upon horseback lashes a beggar on foot
Hurrah for revolution and cannon come again
The beggars have changed places but the lash goes on.

—W. B. Yeats, *The Great Day*

Shortly before the Boer War, Lord Milner remarked, "There is only one way out of the troubles in South Africa: reform or war." Perhaps the obvious has a way of repeating itself, but South Africa today faces a similar dilemma: revolution, armed struggle and internal destruction; or negotiation, bargaining and innovative alternatives that result in the end of apartheid and the start of reconciliation. In many ways the former is easier, less complex and certainly understandable. The latter demands analysis, assessment, creativity and patience.

For South Africans, both white and black, the choice between furthering revolution or participating in reconciliation is a decision that is staring them in the face. That same choice is applicable to North American Christians as we confront various goals and strategies in our efforts to encourage a post-apartheid democratic South Africa. The debate on economic sanctions against South Africa, which has encompassed our political, religious and corporate worlds, is only the first sign of the ultimate dilemma. The questions we must now face move beyond disinvestment and divestment; they examine the choices of armed revolutionary struggle or negotiation and reconciliation. Which policy should one endorse, which strategy support, which alternative pursue?

This book is not an effort to condemn the revolutionary option simply because it involves armed struggle. Nor is it an exercise to condone it because it is the "gospel in praxis." Rather, its purpose is to provide guidelines for realistically considering how to achieve a post-apartheid South Africa which is both just and democratic.

South Africa is one of many historical and current situations which demands consideration of armed revolution as a possible response to injustice. Christian history presents us with a number of different responses to the question of whether force may be used, and if so, under what conditions. These responses can be broadly separated into three categories: pacifism, or an absolute refusal to engage or encourage armed struggle; the crusade or the "holy war," which sanctifies violence; and the "just war," which reluctantly permits the use of force, but only when certain criteria are met and only in pursuit of peace, justice and freedom.

Theoretically and historically pacifism absolutely rejects the use of violence. (Of course, not all who have proclaimed themselves pacifists have been consistently faithful to their principles.) Theologian Peter Brock suggests that pacifism combines "advocacy of personal nonparticipation in war of any kind or in violent revolution with an endeavor to find nonviolent means of resolving conflict."[1] The differences between personal pacifism and corporate or national pacifism have consistently been a topic of discussion within theological and ethical study. *The Challenge of Peace: God's Promise and Our Response,* the 1983 pastoral letter of the National Conference of Catholic Bishops, rejected pacifism as appropriate for governments, yet affirmed it as an option for individual consciences.[2]

Pacifism has historically come in many shades and variations. Strict pacifists hold that war and Christian participation in war are always wrong and violate the norm of neighbor-love and the *imitatio Christi.* Leo Tolstoy, often an advocate of pacifist principles, wrote, "Never resist the evildoer by force, do not meet violence with violence. If they beat you, endure it; if they take your possessions, yield them up. . . ."[3] In the 20th century certain proponents of Christian pacifism seem to be straying from this consistent approach. For example, Philip and Daniel Berrigan have suggested a re-definition of nonviolence, one that would include the possibility of violence against property. Daniel Berrigan has also refused to dismiss the option of violence in certain Third

World revolutionary situations.[4] In recent years it seems that there have been serious compromises in pacifist commitments, which have resulted in something which at best can be called "selective pacifism." Historic pacifists might well view it as "pseudo-pacifism." There have been efforts to suggest that pacifism and the just-war theory are somehow reconcilable. They are not, in fact, parallel traditions, and as George Weigel, a Roman Catholic theologian, has commented, "The integrity of both positions requires that their distinctiveness be maintained."[5] Perhaps the most evident similarity between the two traditions is a common starting line. They both begin with a strong presumption against the use of armed force—beyond that commonality the differences are dramatic.

Another approach to the war and peace dilemma is the medieval notion of a crusade. Historically the "holy war" option was a third attitude toward war that developed, coming after the early pacifist strains in the church and following on the heels of the more dominant and mainstream Augustinian tradition of just-war. Roland Bainton has identified the crusade by four characteristics: holy cause, belief in divine guidance and aid, godly crusaders and ungodly enemies, and unsparing prosecution.[6]

During the Middle Ages the idea of a crusade provided a new answer to the war and peace debate. As Bainton puts it, "Here was a war inaugurated by the Church. Service was volunteered rather than exacted by a ruler from his retainers. . . . There was no residue here of the Augustinian mournfulness in combat. The mood was strangely compounded of barbarian lust for combat and Christian zeal for faith."[7]

The crusade approach was as much an "answer" to 11th- and 12th-century political and ecclesiastical realities as it was to a "new" ethical approach to the dilemma of war and peace. Paul Johnson reminds us: "The idea that Europe was a Christian entity, which had acquired certain inherent rights over the rest of the world by virtue of its faith, and its duty to spread it, married perfectly with the need to find some outlet both for its addiction to violence and its surplus population."[8] Violence at home was the order of the day, so some in the church were quick to channel that violent energy into war "against the foreign infidel." Bainton contends that peace at home was partially to be achieved by diverting bellicosity to a foreign adventure.[9]

(It ought to be acknowledged that many of the original crusaders were not motivated by a desire to shed blood, but by a genuine concern for Christians being persecuted by extremist Moslems. As the Crusades dragged on, however, far less defensible motivations came to dominate.)

The notion of the crusade has clearly been outside the mainstream of church thinking since the medieval period, although it did enjoy a brief resurgence among certain Protestant extremists in the 16th century. In the city of Muenster, for instance, radical churchmen seized control of the municipal government and called for the slaughter of the ungodly. Today, however, elements within the theory of the crusade seem to be making a popular comeback. As George Weigel and others have commented, the crusade notion that war can be a positive moral good and that violence can be redemptive has reemerged among some liberation theologians.

In contrast to pacifism (no war) and the crusade ("holy war") is the tradition that affirms both the right of self-defense and its moral limits, the "just war." The just-war tradition is clearly the mainstream Christian approach to the war and peace debate. The nature of the Christian concept of just war can be viewed both thematically and historically.

Thematically the just-war tradition emerges as a response to the central question: Can a Christian ever justifiably take part in violence?[10] A negative response to the question exemplifies the tradition of pacifism. An affirmative answer demands that a number of corollary questions be asked, defining the conditions and prerequisites that determine when a Christian may resort to violence.

Historically the theory of "just-war" emerged formally with the writings of Ambrose of Milan and particularly Augustine of Hippo in the fourth and fifth centuries. St. Augustine's reflections on war and peace were shaped by the Germanic invasions of the "Christian" Roman Empire. St. Augustine attempted to address ways in which a Christian citizen could participate in defending the Roman Empire. He wrote,

> If Christian teaching forbade war altogether, those looking for the salutary advice of the gospel would have been told to get rid of their arms and give up soldiering. But instead they

were told, "Rob no one by violence or by false accusation, and be content with your wages" (Luke 3:14). If the gospel ordered them to be satisfied with their pay, then it did not forbid a military career.[11]

In addressing ways a Christian citizen could actively participate in the defense of public order, Augustine required that military activities be focused on the ultimate goal of peace, justice and freedom. He wrote, "We do not seek peace in order to wage war, but we go to war to gain peace."[12]

Augustine's outline of a just-war theory was further developed by church thinkers in the 13th century, particularly St. Thomas Aquinas. Beginning to flesh out certain specific questions about power, violence and war, Aquinas wrote in his *Summa Theologiae,*

> Three things are required for any war to be just. The first is the authority of the sovereign on whose command war is waged. . . . Secondly, a just cause is required, namely that those who are attacked are attacked because they deserve it on account of some wrong they have done. . . . Thirdly, the right intention of those waging war is required, that is, they must intend to promote the good and to avoid the evil.[13]

Aquinas concludes with the Augustinian goal of peace, justice and freedom: "Even those who wage a war intend peace. They are not hostile to peace."[14]

Aquinas's late medieval writings expanded upon many of Augustine's earlier notions and ideas. Likewise other medieval, Renaissance and Reformation theologians further refined Aquinas's concepts. These thinkers differentiated between when one could justly go to war—*ad bellum* criteria—and what makes up morally justifiable behavior during war—*in bello* criteria. The 20th-century version of these principles usually focuses on five *ad bellum* criteria and two *in bello* criteria.

Overarching the centuries of the just-war tradition's theoretical development has been the understanding that the goal of applying the theory is one of assuring peace, freedom and justice. None of the just-war theologians ever attempted to establish war as a positive moral good. The just-war tradition rejects any notion of the crusade's "holy war." Augustine's presence is always felt: "We go to war to gain peace." Peace is always the ultimate objective and we resort to war only when it is morally justifiable because it is the lesser of two evils. The norm for Christians is that they pursue peace, justice and freedom. In this pursuit if the criteria for a just war are fulfilled, entering into war is morally justifiable.

There is still wide discussion on the exact wording of the criteria that have come to make up the just-war questions. (The tradition is not doctrine, but rather basic core principles that are subject to refinement.) Typically, the following five *ad bellum* (before war) principles are applied:

(i) There must be a just cause, a real injury that has been suffered;

(ii) War must be declared by a legitimate authority;

(iii) War must be entered into with right intention;

(iv) Violence is the only way left for effecting change;

(v) The war must have a reasonable hope of success.

The criteria usually associated with *in bello* or moral conduct within war are:

(vi) The means must be appropriate to the end (principle of proportionality);

(vii) Reconciliation must be the final end of war.

The just-war tradition is a minimalist tradition. Its criteria are the hurdles that must be faced before a Christian is justified in resorting to violence. The tradition does not glorify or honor war. All of the criteria must be fulfilled. The just-war criteria is not a check list at the end of which the church gladly "blesses" war. Rather the just-war criteria are part of a tradition, a strategy that has as its goal St. Augustine's *tranquillitas ordinis*—the tranquillity of rightly ordered political community.[15]

(i) There must be a just cause, a real injury which has been suffered.

St. Augustine and St. Thomas insisted on this principle to reject trivial motives for instigating violence: sheer revenge, personal power or pure economic gains. In contrast, self-defense would clearly fulfill this criterion.

(ii) War must be declared by a legitimate authority.

Historically this criterion first emerged as a result of medieval theologians' concerns over the ubiquitous battles and wars between the private armies of petty nobility. John Macquarrie writes, "No merely private group is entitled to use violence to tear down the political structure."[16] He suggests that ". . .of all the forms of war and violence, civil disorder is the worst, and rarely achieves that freedom at which it aims."[17] Limiting the just use of violence to "legitimate authorities" reinforces the critical nature of legal and political institutions. It reminds us that it is via these institutions that conflict can best be avoided.

(iii) War must be entered into with right intention.

Aquinas laid the groundwork for this principle when he wrote, "The right intention of those waging war is required, that is, they must intend to promote the good and to avoid evil."[18] What are determined to be "good" intentions or "evil" intentions are, of course, to some degree a matter of subjective interpretation. Adolf Hitler insisted that he was going to war to "promote the good." Goals and intentions, however, must be measured against the traditional Christian values of justice, freedom and peace.

(iv) Resorting to violence must be the only way left to effect change.

John Macquarrie suggests, "There is a tendency to hasten to the use of violence long before it can be legitimately considered a last resort."[19] This principle demands that only after all other means have been used to the fullest extent and failed is there any excuse for violence. These other channels include various forms of political negotiations, economic boycotts, litigation and all other nonviolent pressures. Macquarrie notes,

> This means that violence is never justified in states where legal political channels are open, and where there is reasonable freedom of action. Only where every nonviolent way of redress is denied can violence be considered acceptable.[20]

(v) The war must have a reasonable hope of success.

"Or what king, going to encounter another king in war, will not sit down first and take council whether he is able with ten thousand to meet him who comes against him with twenty thousand" (Luke 14:31). To enter into violence without a reasonable chance of accomplishing your intentions is not a morally justifiable action. Macquarrie writes, "Such forms of violence correspond to suicide in an individual. They amount to a total denial of hope."[21] They, in fact, point to a cavalier, unchristian attitude towards human suffering and death.

For centuries these five "ad bellum" criteria have been the accepted norm within the Christian church to assist us in determining when violence is justifiable. This is not to deny the existence or intellectual importance of the pacifist and crusade approaches to the war/peace debate. However, it is a central thesis of this book that the 20th century will be well served if Christians take seriously the church's just-war tradition in determining when they are permitted, or perhaps even compelled, to resort to violence in the pursuit of peace, freedom and justice.

The Just-War Tradition and Revolution

The just-war tradition has historically been understood and used in analyzing war between two or more sovereign states. However, the concept of a justifiable revolution also has had a place, at least implicitly, in the church's discussion of the just use of violence. Thematically, the just-war tradition's central question is, "Under what conditions may a Christian justifiably take part in violence?" Violence, of course, can be interstate or intrastate. There is no explicit "just-revolution" theory; hence it is appropriate and necessary to look to the just-war tradition for moral guidance concerning when it is justifiable for Christians to enter into revolution. The just-war tradition evolved because of a desire to address the moral dilemma of when violence was permissible and when it was not. The need to apply the tradition and principles is no less important for internal war (revolution) than for war between sovereign nations.

The church has historically held a positive view of the function of government in society. According to tradition, God in his providence intends there to be a structure of government for the ordering of the body politic; this ordering results in a benefit to all in society. However, the state's authority is conditioned upon its fulfilling the purpose for which it was ordained by God. The state ought not to become absolute. In the earthly city, as St. Augustine reminds us, there are times when the state authorities lose sight of their true purpose. They ignore why they were ordained and by whom. When does it become justifiable, we must ask, for Christians to enter into violent revolution and attempt to overthrow the existing political institutions in power?

The five *ad bellum* criteria of the just-war tradition clearly have certain limitations when applied to a pre-revolutionary situation. They do, however, provide the most complete and traditionally accepted guidelines by which Christians can assess the questions of armed revolution. Overall there is not a better resource than the just-war tradition for providing us with historical and moral criteria for evaluating violent revolution.

A caveat must be noted concerning the modern understanding of "revolution." Aquinas's understanding of revolt and rebellion is clearly different from the common 20th-century concept of revolution. Traditional ideas of resistance to tyranny are quite distant from the modern social theory of revolution. Traditionally rebellion against tyranny (specifically armed struggle) is undertaken to restore a previously established but temporarily lost legitimate government. Civil strife, like war between two sovereigns, must be entered into cautiously. The modern notion of revolution, however, increasingly has held that the revolutionaries are creating something genuinely new in history, not simply correcting abuses of a previous regime. The French Revolution, in part, initiated this modern understanding, but it was Marx, in his use of the Hegelian dialectic, who developed a distinctive modern revolutionary theory. (The American Revolution, in contrast, was somewhat closer to the medieval notion of rebellion against tyranny than to the modern understanding of revolutionary transformation. To be sure, however, even here there was a self-conscious sense of embarking on a "new" experiment. But it was a "new" experiment with clear historical roots and precedents.)

The fact that the modern understanding of revolution is at variance with that of the pre-modern era does not mean that just-war principles are now obsolete. However, the glaring differences between the traditional Christian understanding of revolt and the Marxist-Leninist notion of revolution is critical to keep in mind as we seek to apply just-war criteria to modern revolutionary settings.[22]

The five *ad bellum* principles can be applied to a revolutionary environment as follows:

(i) The revolution must have a just cause involving a real injury.

As in the case of war, entering into violence must be precipitated by real injury. The injury inflicted must be borne by significant portions of society. Determining "just cause" or real injury can often turn into a highly subjective exercise. Richard John Neuhaus has warned, "One person's real injury is another person's minor inconvenience."[23] For this criterion to be fulfilled, a government must consistently institutionalize injustices and restrain freedoms, causing real injury to the people it claims to represent. If that is the case, then the regime can no longer be viewed as the legitimate authority.

(ii) Revolution must be led by a properly constituted authority.

According to Macquarrie, "No merely private group is entitled to use violence to tear down the political structure. (It) should be remembered that of all the forms of war and violence, civil disorder is the worst, and rarely achieves that freedom at which it aims."[24] In light of this, it is crucial that we understand what "legitimate authority" means.

In a revolutionary scenario, revolutionary elites are in fact vying for this "legitimate authority" label against the existing government. Any existing regime, legitimate or not, is going to seek to discredit a revolutionary movement's attempts to gain legitimacy. Legitimacy labels will be based upon national (internal), regional and international recognition and support. In granting a revolutionary group the "legitimate authority" recognition, it is implied that the existing government is, in fact, illegitimate.

(iii) Revolution must be entered into with right intention.

To extend this principle from a just-war to a just-revolution criterion requires the revolutionary elite to enunciate its intentions and visions for the future. St. Thomas's notion of promoting "good" remains at the core of this concept. "The right intention of those waging war is required, that is, they must intend to promote the good and to avoid evil."[25] This third criterion addresses the dilemma that many revolutions have faced: will the oppressed simply become the new oppressors? Even Daniel Berrigan once wrote, "A revolution is interesting insofar as it avoids like the plague the plague it promises to heal."[26]

It is in this third principle that serious theoretical and practical conflicts become apparent between Marxist-Leninist revolutionary concepts and the just-war tradition. Frequently, the Marxist-Leninists have defined revolution as "a dynamic condition in a man's relation to social existence."[27] For some Marxist-Leninist theorists, there is no other goal than "liberation from existing structures."[28] The ultimate intentions and goals of a revolution are alleged to be concerns of another day. According to this thinking, what the revolutionary will do with his power when he has established his humanity is a later and secondary question. First he must rebel, the theory suggests, and in this rebellion a new community will rise.

The "revolution first, goals second" mentality attempts to excuse the lack of a post-revolutionary agenda. Via the revolution, the logic proceeds, man and his potential is revealed and a unique, greater order will emerge from blood and ashes. As Richard John Neuhaus suggests, this phenomenon "is a faith worthy of a mystic. It is a religion; violence and talk of violence is its sacrament. The suspension of intelligence is the only fee required for invitation into the fellowship of the revolutionary elect."[29]

The third criterion requires a thorough examination of a revolutionary movement's aspirations and intentions, an assessment that is faithful to Aquinas's notion of "promoting the good and avoiding the evil."

(iv) Revolutionary violence must be the only way left to effect change.

This fourth principle is applicable to a revolutionary environment in that it addresses the use of nonviolent means to cause change. In an intrastate conflict, legal, political, economic and other nonviolent pressures must be used to the fullest extent before it is morally justifiable to resort to violence.

Similar to military governments, revolutionary elites are often quick to embrace armed struggle. The Leninist notion of revolution as the conduit of the proletariat's conscientization process is directly opposed to this fourth principle. In Lenin there is no call to utilize violence only as a last resort; on the contrary, armed revolution is an early and preferred course of action. The central question for the Leninist is, "Will violence be successful at a given historical moment?"

Discerning whether all nonviolent efforts have been undertaken and blocked can be a subjective and difficult task. A key method for assisting us in determining whether all avenues of change have been obstructed is to examine what, if any, changes have occurred in the society as a result of nonviolent pressure.

(v) The revolution must have a reasonable hope of success.

In a revolutionary setting, measuring "hope of success" is an undertaking that requires some understanding of military power as well as an ability to forecast the potential for "mobilization" of the populace. It is often more difficult to assess a revolutionary movement's military potential and the mass mobilization factor (vis-à-vis the existing regime's power) than it is to assess the military capabilities of two potentially belligerent sovereign states. However, the possibilities and probabilities of a revolution succeeding can be estimated and tentative conclusions drawn.

A warning must be mentioned concerning the data and material used for assessing this fifth criterion. The information concerning the strengths and weaknesses of a revolutionary group, as well as the existing government, will naturally be a matter of considerable debate. There have been few revolutionary militia commanders who have not predicted an inevitable, and often quick, victory. Likewise commanding generals of standing armies rarely acknowledge that a revolutionary group might have "a reasonable hope of success."

Although just-war criteria require some fine tuning for application to revolutionary situations, they are still by far the best means available for dealing with the traditional Christian concerns for peace, justice and freedom.

Revolution and South Africa

The just-war tradition is a living tradition, one that is relevant to our late twentieth century and one that should be examined with regard to numerous war/peace issues and policies. South Africa is one such example where a thorough study of the situation can be made using the just-war criteria.

It has become a cliché to claim that we live in an age of revolution, and it has recently been suggested that the cliché might be evolving into an anachronism. But the coals of revolution are being stoked in southern Africa. To claim that the revolution is well under way in South Africa is premature. For some it is simply wishful thinking. The sparks of revolution flicker, however, and could well be fanned into engulfing flames. Writing about South Africa in 1987, William Raspberry expressed the frustration of many: "It's hard to see anything short of full scale revolution that offers even a glimmer of hope for a solution."[30] However, violent revolution in South Africa is not inevitable, though it cannot be denied that the conditions for violent upheaval are, and have been, present for some time. A South African political scientist and self-described Marxist recently said,

> I advise you not to listen to people who give you wise-

sounding reasons about why there will not be revolution here. Revolution is not something you calculate, it's something you smell, and I smell it in the air.[31]

Though the "smell" of revolution may be in the air for some, a full-scale revolution is not underway in South Africa, and so the *ad bellum* criteria will be the focus of our attention. How long that odor lingers and how strong it becomes will depend on numerous internal, regional and international developments. How North American Christians perceive and respond to the South African scenario will partially influence the future of that nation and the southern African subcontinent.

The potential South African revolutionary situation provides more than a case study for the just-war tradition. More importantly the just-war theory provides a method by which Christians concerned about democracy and human rights can assess the current realities in South Africa and come to conclusions on which course of action to follow: maintaining the status quo, fomenting revolution or supporting reform alternatives with real potential to promote peace, freedom and justice.

Two

Revolution Due to Injury

A just cause is required, namely that those who are attacked are attacked because they deserve it on account of some wrong they have done.[1]

—St. Thomas Aquinas

The first criterion focuses on the existing regime and its governing of its people. In any revolutionary scenario, this criterion is fulfilled when the government in power causes real injury to the very people it claims to represent, and therefore constitutes an "illegitimate government." The "injury" in question must be systematic and universal, not occasional or accidental.

Determining what constitutes an "injury" is clearly a subjective task that may be used by either the revolutionary elite attempting to gain recognition, or the existing regime attempting to discredit the challenger. The following assessment of the injuries incurred by the people of South Africa is based upon a democratic, liberal and Christian perspective.

An integral part of analyzing "real injury" is looking at specifics. A frequent fault of revolutionary movements is that instead of examining specific injuries, they tend to generalize and categorize the existing regime as totally and completely oppressive. (In certain instances, it should be noted, governments are indeed thoroughly oppressive.) This generalization process leads to the often inaccurate conclusion that absolutely nothing positive can emerge from the existing government. If anything that resembles a positive step is produced, so the theory goes, it is only a facade hiding the sinister oppression of the regime.[2] In an attempt to assess how the South African government is accountable to its citizens and how the Pretoria regime uses its power, it is necessary to look at specific injuries: who is injured, how they are injured and the frequency and gravity of the injuries.

The South African Government's Accountability

"May 6, 1987 witnessed a democratic election in South Africa." That statement is quite correct on one level but reveals a very "real injury" on another. The election did, in fact, have a voter turnout of more than 70 percent of the registered voters. The injury in this quasi-democratic process is that only 20 percent of the population was registered to vote. The black population in South Africa does not have representation in Parliament. (There are nominal voting rights for blacks in the "independent homelands" and for some local elections.) The Indian and "coloured" populations were extended certain voting rights for their separate chambers of Parliament in 1983. This limited parliamentary representation provided under the constitutional changes of 1983 has been highly criticized and, in fact, was a primary stimulus for the violence which began in 1984 and led to the State of Emergency. Perhaps Bishop Desmond Tutu's standard stump speech best illustrates the real injury: "Here I stand," he announces, "an Archbishop of the Anglican Church, a Nobel Peace Prize winner, a thoroughly educated, property owning family man, 'citizen' of South Africa, and yet I cannot vote."[3]

To whom is the South African government ultimately accountable? Pretoria claims that it represents all "citizens," black and white, Indian and coloured, of South Africa. The "independent homelands," the official state policy reads, represent and have authority over their residents, although since the early 1980s the Pretoria government has been accepting many urban blacks as South African "citizens." In reality, however, the only people to whom the Pretoria regime is accountable are the white voting public. The black population has no voice in government; it is a population that is unrepresented in Parliament, denied political rights and relegated, in political terms, to a second-class status. The social, economic and cultural aspects of this power structure manifest themselves in apartheid strategies and laws, but the political dimension goes far beyond "separate development"; it goes to the very heart of who rules. This is not to diminish the injury that occurs in the daily lives of South Africans because of apartheid legislation and practices. The ultimate motivation for apartheid, however, is the maintenance of power.

How Pretoria Uses Its Power

Hendrick Verwoerd, along with Ben Schumann and others, constructed in the 1940s and early 1950s a public policy of separate development—apartheid. Verwoerd, trained in psychology and sociology, reasoned that homogeneous populations were more governable than heterogeneous. Hence, to divide a multi-ethnic society into smaller homogeneous societies would prove to be a more efficient structure for governing. The scheme has failed politically, socially and economically. At the core of apartheid is the Population Registration Act of 1950. Upon this law, which requires all people to be classified into certain racial categories, rest all subsequent apartheid legislation. The Group Areas Act determines where racial groups may or may not reside, and education legislation restricts where children go to school (and often whether they get any education at all). Recently two pillars of apartheid were altered: the infamous pass laws, or Influx Control, which restricted where blacks could travel and work; and Job Reservation laws, which reserved certain employment opportunities for whites only. (The "reform" efforts will be studied in chapter five.)

One particularly insidious injury that results from the Group Areas Act is forced removals. The government has, in the past, forced black families to abandon their small makeshift homes and shacks to be transported to the homelands, often hundreds of miles away. The government has frequently offered minimal assistance in the move, and then ordered bulldozers to raze the homes. Since the 1950s it is estimated that more than 125,000 families have been forced to move because of the Group Areas Act. Forced removals have slowed considerably in the recent past, yet the Group Areas Act still remains in effect.

The canonization of apartheid into official legislation results in specific and consistent injury to many South Africans. In response to this legislation, many blacks, whites, Indians and coloreds have attempted to demonstrate the unacceptability of such discrimination. In a cyclical fashion, the government has further clamped down on dissent. On July 12, 1986, P.W. Botha imposed a nationwide State of Emergency which prohibited: 1) "any campaign project or action aimed at accomplishing the release of persons already detained"; 2) signing or supporting any petitions calling for the release of detainees; 3) the exhibition in public of any clothing, sticker or poster "protesting against or disapproving of detentions"; 4) the attending of any gathering protesting detention or honoring detainees. Other State of Emergency stipulations severely restrict the press, both foreign and domestic. In June 1989, the State of Emergency was officially extended for a fourth year.

The widespread practice of detaining individuals, often with no charges immediately brought against them, has emerged as a clear example of abuse of government power. In early February 1987 the South African government released "official figures" that put at 13,500 the number of detainees who had been held for more than a month since the State of Emergency was declared in June 1986. The official numbers also listed 281 children who had been detained since June 1987. ("Children" were defined as under 18 years of age.)[4] The Detainees Parents Support Committee released its findings also in early February 1987, which placed the numbers of detainees at 25,000 since June 1986. By all accounts the number of detainees had dropped significantly by 1989. The South African Council of Churches estimated that there were under 50 detainees as of May 1989.[5] The exact numbers are not entirely certain, but the injury incurred is quite real. This is not to conclude, however, that all of those arrested and detained were innocent of being involved in dangerous and injurious activities which might require detention. Undoubtedly, some of those detained could be convicted for their roles in violent acts. The real injury, however, comes with the breach in the due process of law. When individuals are held for months at a time without having charges made against them, the government has clearly abused its power.

In a show of force, itself illustrative of waning legitimacy, the South African government has deployed large numbers of police and army units in the townships since the State of Emergency was imposed. Estimates indicate that as much as 80 percent of the country's 35,000-strong police force is now in the townships.[6] In 1986 it was not uncommon for black schools to be under occupation by armed police or soldiers.

"Occupation" of the townships and massive detentions signal abuse of power, but the number of deaths since the State of Emergency reinforces the "smell of revolution." According to the Secretary of State's Advisory Committee on South Africa, between September 1984 and January 1987 more than 2,200 people were killed. The majority of those deaths was at the hands of security forces. However, these violent deaths also include the insidious "necklacing" deaths that result from "black on black" violence, all of which increase a revolutionary psychology within the townships. During the height of the 1984 to 1986 violence, an entire generation of black youths were out of school, in some instances as long as two years. Those youngsters have undoubtedly been radicalized by witnessing daily shootings, burnings, jailings and possible torture.

In South Africa today there is a consistent and systematic practice that causes real injury to the very citizens the regime supposedly represents. In the final assessment, the South African government is only accountable to the 20 percent of the population that happens to have white skin. Eighty percent are unrepresented and hence have no real political power. South Africa is only a "quasi-democracy," and such a democratic facade cannot claim full, legitimate authority. What perhaps remains as one of South Africa's most frustrating characteristics is a seemingly democratic structure, with division of powers, checks and balances and regular elections. This democratic structure, unfortunately, is only operated by and functions for a racial elite—not the nation's total citizenry.

From a post-Enlightenment, Western perspective, the notion of governmental legitimacy has become increasingly identified with the notion of constitutionality. The concept of constitutionality has often been identified with democratic values, including the concept of checks and balances within a government structure. This is not to suggest that any government with a constitution has a democratic ethos that permeates and guides the government and society. (There are numerous nations, currently and in history, that officially embrace a constitution but in fact ignore democracy.) But a constitutionally elected government does have one foot in the "legitimate" camp.

The dilemma concerning the South African government's "legitimacy" centers not so much around its constitutional checks and balances, but its deliberate and legal electoral exclusion of 80 percent of the population. For the voting 20 percent, the South African government could be considered quite legitimate. Can the same be said for the non-voting 80 percent? In the South African context, the lack of democratic practices, the abuse of power and the real injury caused by the Pretoria regime point to a government that does not truly represent most of its people. Thus it is in many respects morally illegitimate. Does this then imply that there is automatically a morally legitimate government-in-waiting? Or that any revolutionary elite calling for the overthrow of an illegitimate regime is by fiat "legitimate" in its own right? Clearly the answer is no, and that is why the just-war tradition asks the critical question, "Is the revolution being led by a legitimate authority?"

Three

Revolution by a Legitimate Authority

Obviously, the "people" is not one person and one voice but a heterogeneous crowd of individuals making cacophonous noises. Where then is legitimacy to be found?[1]

—Richard John Neuhaus

The Organization of African Unity (OAU) determines whether a "national liberation movement" is legitimate by measuring criteria such as "effective and efficient struggle" and "capacity to represent the population."[2] "Representing the people" in the post-Enlightenment, Western tradition has come to be the yardstick of legitimacy for any group. Jean-Jacques Rousseau defined a legitimate government as one that is responsive to "the general will" of the people. The same can be applied to a revolutionary movement. But how can the "general will" of a people be measured if the measuring stick—free and fair elections—is nonexistent?

The legitimacy of a revolutionary movement can only be assessed as a matter of degree. The question becomes: to what degree are those initiating the revolution truly representative of the interests and aspirations of the populace as a whole? Revolutions do not occur as a result of a simple majority vote or the plurality of an electoral college. Revolutions usually are declared by an elite, a cadre of men and women who form the leadership of a movement. It is this leadership group, or power elite, which must be examined and studied, for they are guiding, directing and motivating the revolution.

Contemporary revolutionary (Marxist) theory recognizes the difficulty in maintaining a relationship between the people and a revolutionary movement. The "revolutionary elite" become the critical link between the masses and the movement. To prove legitimacy the revolutionary elite will attempt to convince all who are willing to listen that they are the conduit for a higher good. Hence the "revolutionary elite," or the leadership of a revolution, must be analyzed and assessed if a revolutionary movement is to be understood.

In this chapter the revolutionary elites who are calling for an armed struggle in South Africa will be identified. (The revolutionary authorities' ultimate goals and intentions will be examined in chapter four.) The African National Congress (ANC) emerges as a critical representative of some of the people in South Africa; hence its international support as well as its domestic (internal) strength will be closely examined.

Who is Calling for Revolution?

Before analyzing to what degree a revolutionary elite is legitimate, it must first be determined if they are, in fact, revolutionary. What are the elites, the associations, the groups —formal and informal—that are calling for change? And which ones, then, specifically advocate an armed struggle?

African National Congress

The African National Congress, founded in 1912 and banned since 1960, is devoted to overthrowing the Pretoria government via an armed revolution. Oliver Tambo, President of the ANC, stated in January 1987, "The objective to transform our armed offensive into a people's war remains one that we must pursue with the greatest vigor."[3] In further defining "people's war," Tambo suggests that "the central task that faces us is to mount the most concerted assault on the apartheid regime. . . . To do this, we require large political and military forces that are united politically and organizationally. To accomplish this goal, we must transform every black urban and rural area into a strong revolutionary base."[4]

To fulfill the policies of an armed revolt, the ANC formed the Umkhonto we Sizwe (Spear of the Nation) in 1963. Joe Slovo, Chairman of the South African Communist Party, was until recently also Chief of Staff of the Umkhonto. The Umkhonto we Sizwe, or the MK, trains guerrillas with the assistance of East-bloc and Soviet advisors in camps in Tanzania, Zambia and, until the recent Angolan-Namibian peace initiative, Angola. Advanced guerrilla recruits may be given specialized training sessions in Bulgaria, Czechoslovakia or the Soviet Union. The MK has steadily increased the number of targets within South Africa. Originally centered on military and strategic industrial sites and installations, the ANC now hits "soft targets" including fast food restaurants and supermarkets.

The ANC leadership appears to be heavily committed to armed struggle. In an interview in the United States, Oliver Tambo admitted that "the renunciation of violence really amounts to surrender on our part."[5] In a December 1986 speech Tambo told the leaders of the MK how critical their efforts were,

> Our people have only been taken seriously, whether in Pretoria, London, Washington, or Bonn, because of our armed activity. Combatants of MK, you are the guarantors of our future; without you our people and the leader of our revolution, the ANC, would be a voice without force. Our history has taught that people's power cannot come through a change of heart from the rulers.[6]

South African Communist Party

The South African Communist Party, banned for more than 25 years, is a small and seemingly insignificant outlawed extra-parliamentary group. Its importance and power does not rest with its numbers of members; it does not have a mass following. Its influence, according to the U.S. State Department, "is through its alliance with the African National Congress. The SACP continues to view its historical alliance with the ANC as its main hope for winning power in South Africa."[7]

The SACP clearly adheres to the Marxist understanding of an armed revolution. It anticipates a two-stage revolution that consists of a "nationalist" revolution that is followed by a second stage that ushers in the classless society. (A closer examination of the SACP's goals is found in chapter four.)

In 1962 the SACP formulated its revolutionary theory that remains authoritative today: "The first stage of the revolution is to build a unified front of national liberation (primarily African liberation) that would unite all sections and classes."[8] Eventually the second stage of the revolution would emerge, "one to advance the establishment of a socialist South Africa, laying the foundations of a classless, communist society."[9]

The SACP's revolutionary goals and aspirations are backed up with its concrete ties with the Soviet Union. According to Ken Owen, editor of *Business Day* newspaper in Johannesburg, "The SACP is the most devoted, pro-Soviet communist party in all of Africa and perhaps the world."[10] In the past, the SACP-Moscow link has reaped real dividends for the armed struggle. According to the U.S. State Department the SACP-ANC alliance has "near total dependence on the Soviet bloc for military assistance."[11] Armed by the Eastern bloc, the SACP-ANC alliance represents the most organized and sophisticated group calling for revolution.

United Democratic Front

The United Democratic Front is an umbrella organization that represents a coalition of some 600 to 700 organizations that include political, community, labor, religious and youth groups. Founded in 1983 in reaction to the new constitution that created "coloured" and "Indian" chambers in Parliament, the UDF represents a broad ethnic, geographic and demographic base. Since the State of Emergency was declared in 1986, numerous UDF leaders have been detained. In early 1988 a number of UDF leaders were banned.

Officially not tied with the ANC, the UDF has endorsed the ANC's primary manifesto, the Freedom Charter (see chapter four). Writing for *The Nation*, Mike Calabrese states, "The 1.5 million-member UDF is led primarily by former ANC activists; its 600 youth and community groups have endorsed the Freedom Charter."[12] The UDF does not advocate armed struggle, but its political orientation does seem strongly to mirror that of the ANC.

Roman Catholic Archbishop Denis Hurley of Durban describes the UDF's strategy as a "politics of confrontation with a view to negotiating at the top level only."[13] However in July 1987, Murphy Morobe, the UDF's publicity secretary, rejected the possibility of any talks between the government and his organization.[14] Unlike the ANC, an open call for armed revolution is not the UDF's strategy or tactic. However, "the political attitudes of the UDF and the ANC are the same," explains Archbishop Hurley, "apart from the questions of violence."

Labor Unions

Black unions, legalized in 1979, have seen rapid growth both in membership and in economic and political leverage. In 1979 there were some 30,000 black union members. By the end of 1987 their numbers had increased to nearly one million, which represents nine percent of the work force in South Africa.[15]

The largest trade union association, formed in 1985, is the Confederation of South African Trade Unions (COSATU), which claims a membership of more than 800,000. The second largest union, Council of Unions in South Africa (CUSA) merged with the Azanian Confederation of Trade Unions (AZACTU) to form the new National Council of Trade Unions (NACTU), which claims more than 300,000 members. In May 1986 the United Workers Union of South Africa (UWUSA) was organized and now lists 100,000 members.

COSATU has emerged as the most politically active of all of the trade organizations. COSATU is a federation of some 25 unions, including the National Union of Mineworkers (NUM), and because of this broad-based association, maintains links with a wide range of political organizations. In March 1986 COSATU and the ANC had a meeting in Lusaka, Zambia and released a joint communique that summarized the discussions.

> There was a common understanding . . . that lasting solutions can only emerge from the national liberation, headed by the African National Congress(ANC), and the entire democratic forces, of which COSATU is an important and integral part.[16]

The joint ANC-COSATU communique went on to say that both organizations strongly criticize "the apartheid system of national oppression and class exploitation."[17]

Like the UDF, COSATU and other unions have not called for an armed revolution. COSATU has adopted the Freedom Charter as "a guiding document" and has pledged "to teach its people the basic tenets of the Freedom Charter."[18] The ANC particularly views COSATU as a key ally; in an address to the South African Communist Party in 1986 in London, ANC leader Alfred Nzo said,

> "The black working class, the backbone of this movement, has raised its struggle to a high point. . . . The newly

established Congress of South African Trade Unions (COSATU) towers at the head of the workers' revolution.[19]

COSATU's President, Elijah Barayi, has frequently articulated economic policies that tend to analyze social and economic problems in very "class-conscious" terms. He has endorsed policies of nationalization and expropriation.

> Black people are the ones digging gold and in return they are paid peanuts. Once we nationalize the whole industry, our belief is that everyone will reap the fruits of his sweat and toil, rather than a few individuals getting it all for themselves. . . . I believe COSATU is a socialist organization and I would like to see a socialist State in South Africa. . . . This country is in a crisis because of capitalism; if we at least nationalize the big firms, then the government could look after its people and the people could look after the government.[20]

Black Consciousness Movement

In July 1959 a group within the ANC broke off and formed the Pan Africanist Congress (PAC). The first PAC leaders were motivated to make the break from the ANC because they perceived the ANC as straying from its true African nationalist goals and aspirations. This initial "black consciousness" movement was leery of white participation within the ANC, particularly the apparently growing influence the white-dominated South African Communist Party had upon key leadership within the ANC. "The overriding commitment of the PAC was to a purified form of African nationalism," explains the Report of the U.S. Secretary of State's Advisory Committee on South Africa.[21]

On April 8, 1960, the South African government banned both the ANC and the PAC. Since then the PAC has not had nearly the success that the ANC has had in maintaining an exile apparatus with offices and personnel positioned throughout the world. Although the PAC still functions and has its headquarters in Dar es Salaam, Tanzania, the torch of the black consciousness movement seems to have passed to a group that has its roots in the PAC, the Azanian People's Organization, or AZAPO.

Formed in 1978 by black intellectuals, AZAPO appears to carry the traditions of the socialists, yet somewhat leery of Marxists and communists, and fervently nationalistic in a peculiarly African sense. Some AZAPO leaders have attempted to define their understanding of "black" nationalism as meaning "anyone who owes allegiance to Africa, whatever the complexion of his skin."[22] Even if a person is black, goes the logic, he ceases to be "black" if he supports a "non-black faction" (read ANC). These nuances are not always apparent to the rank and file, and frequently the black consciousness ideals take on a racist tone.

The specifics of the PAC's and AZAPO's strategy for armed revolution are not entirely clear, but it is quite evident that the leadership believes in and adheres to a strategy of revolution led by African nationalists. This is in direct conflict with the ANC's alliance with the white-dominated SACP. PAC Chairman Johnson Mlampo in May 1987 stated, "The most effective method of struggle is armed struggle."[23] AZAPO and the black consciousness movement's ultimate goal is a truly African South Africa whose name will be Azania. Azania will be the result of a struggle that will, they perceive, entail revolutionary violence.

Inkatha

In 1974 the Chief Minister Of Kwazulu, Mangosuthu Buthelezi, revived a Zulu cultural organization founded in 1928 known as "Inkatha." Chief "Gatsha" Buthelezi's Inkatha is frequently described as the largest legal black political organization in the country, with more than one million members.

Chief Buthelezi rejects armed struggle, though he remains an advocate of "radical change" within his country. Buthelezi and Inkatha preach against violent revolution, yet they refuse to begin negotiations with the South African regime until certain conditions are met (the release of ANC leader Nelson Mandela being a primary demand). Inkatha's relations with the ANC have been strained since 1980, and violent clashes between the UDF and Inkatha have erupted in Natal, Inkatha's geographic base.

Buthelezi has stated that Inkatha demands "a radical revision of basic values and attitudes among white South Africans. . .We reject the racist foundations on which not only the constitution but so many of these institutions in South Africa are based."[24] Yet, according to Inkatha, violent revolution is not the way to reach the goal of a truly democratic, post-apartheid South Africa. Buthelezi stated, "I say clearly to the world that black South Africans will not turn to supporting violence en masse while there is yet one nonviolent action which would succeed."[25]

Afrikaner Weerstandsbeweging

The Afrikaner Weerstandsbeweging (AWB), or Afrikaner Resistance Movement, represents the threat of revolution from the extreme Right on the political spectrum. Formed in the early 1980s, the AWB is a paramilitary organization that resists any reforms in the apartheid structure and calls for a nearly complete separation of the races. The AWB, led by Eugene Terre Blanche, finds its strength primarily in small towns and rural areas, particularly in the Transvaal.

Although the AWB is highly critical of the Nationalist Party and the current South African government, it has not called for an armed revolution. It has pledged its political and military clout in resisting any "power-sharing" schemes that would lead directly to black rule.

Defining and determining exactly who is "revolutionary" (calling for an armed revolution) is the first step in assessing the legitimacy of a revolutionary elite. That assessment is perhaps more difficult than it initially might appear. Considering the seven organizations described above (there certainly are other extra-parliamentary political groups, but the ones outlined represent the largest and most developed), only the ANC-SACP alliance and PAC have an unambiguous position supporting an armed revolution. The UDF, which often echoes ANC thinking, does not openly endorse a revolution at this time, nor do any labor unions, although the COSATU-ANC communique demonstrates a working arrangement between a revolutionary elite and a nonviolent trade union (see chapter 12). Inkatha goes out of its way to emphasize its "nonviolent" strategy, yet it has been known to carry out repressive, often violent acts against other groups. However, Inkatha has never openly called for an armed revolution against the existing regime.

The AWB has expressed the possibility of an armed revolt but never issued a direct call against the Pretoria government.

The remainder of this chapter will focus on the largest and most externally developed revolutionary elite, the African National Congress. This in itself is perhaps lending "legitimacy" to the ANC, yet to deny the ANC the status of a "revolutionary elite," is to deny the reality of the South African situation in the late 1980s.

ANC: The 'Leading' Revolutionary Elite

The ANC is different things to different people. According to Joseph Lelyveld, a long-time South Africa watcher and *New York Times* writer, "The ANC shows different faces in different forums."[26] At the 1983 World Council of Churches meeting in Vancouver, the ANC described itself as "a community of love and justice on a pilgrim road to freedom."[27] A few months later over the ANC radio, based in Ethiopia and Angola and known as "Radio Freedom," the ANC broadcast the importance of the armed struggle.

> . . . it is the military victories on the ground, the stinging blows delivered by our heroic combatants and our death-defying workers and youth in the dusty streets of our townships that are finally going to drive out the apartheid rulers.[28]

Founded in 1912 as the African Native National Congress, the early nationalist group embraced expressly moderate views, strategies and tactics. In 1955 the ANC adopted the Freedom Charter as its primary manifesto, written by a consortium of nationalists and communists. After the Sharpeville massacre, the ANC (along with the PAC and the SACP) was banned on April 8, 1960, under the Unlawful Organization Act. Since 1960 the ANC has been an exiled group that, until recently, has steadily increased its commitment to an armed revolution. (For an in-depth study of ANC intentions and strategies see chapter 5.) "Incidents of terrorism," as the South African government calls them, have increased from 44 in 1984, to 136 in 1985, to 170 in the first nine months of 1986. By late 1988, however, the incidents declined.[29]

The South African Government claims that there are fewer than 100 trained ANC guerrillas inside South Africa at any one time. Professor Tom Lodge of the University of Witswatersrand, a leading authority on the ANC who has excellent contact with the ANC leadership both in exile and inside South Africa, suggests that the ANC has approximately 500 military operatives within South Africa and an external army of 12,000 to 15,000.[30] The CIA has estimated that there are up to 2,000 guerrillas in South Africa and 8,000 to 10,000 being trained in camps in Angola, Tanzania, Zambia and the Eastern bloc.[31]

The ANC views itself as a non-racial, non-tribal revolutionary movement, pursuing a "united, democratic South Africa." Yet a substantial proportion (exact numbers are unavailable) of the ANC membership list is Xhosa. Tom Lodge and others explain that the ANC has traditionally recruited from the Eastern Cape, a predominantly Xhosa area. (Lodge suggested that tribal identities within the ANC surface particularly during difficult times and are focused generally on secondary issues.)

What are the factors that would contribute to making the ANC a "legitimate authority"? On an international level it is critical to note and assess which sovereign nations recognize and/or support this revolutionary elite and what its standing is in multinational forums such as the United Nations. On a domestic level what other organizations support the ANC and how they support it must also be examined. The "measuring stick" of free elections is unavailable; therefore other methods of determining "grassroots" or popular support must be utilized.

International Acknowledgment, Recognition and Support

The West

On January 28, 1987 ANC President Oliver Tambo arrived at the State Department for a day-long meeting with U.S. officials, including Secretary of State George Shultz. It was the first meeting between an ANC leader and a U.S. cabinet official. After the meeting a State Department spokesman explained the Reagan Administration's policy toward the ANC: "The policy of our government is to expand our contacts with the ANC—partly to test them to see what is the nature of its make-up and to state to them forcefully U.S. positions on violence."[32]

There is an obvious difference between recognizing the existence of a revolutionary movement and supporting it. There is also a more subtle, yet significant, distinction between "recognition" and what might be called "acknowledgment" of a revolutionary elite. The official U.S. policy seems to be that of acknowledgment—that the ANC is one element within South Africa that must be consulted—rather than any official recognition. (Recognition implies an official agreement with, if not support of, a group.)

Other Western nations (United Kingdom, West Germany, France and Japan, for example) have "acknowledged" the ANC via

high-level meetings and consultations. The ANC maintains offices
in 28 countries throughout the world. Other Western nations clearly recognize and even financially support the ANC. The Scan-
dinavian nations, for instance, often contribute financial resources,
recently up to as much as $20 million annually. The ANC also
receives funds and material aid from the Canadian, Austrian and
Italian governments.[33]

International recognition and support, particularly by Western
nations, has become an important priority for the ANC. Frank
Martin, a former Natal provincial official, explained, "The ANC is
a highly respected group, but their greatest achievement has been
developing a mystique, particularly in international circles, that
they are the sole authentic voice of the black man in South
Africa."[34]

Western non-governmental bodies have also contributed to the
ANC's recognition and support within the international community. The World Council of Churches gives annually to the ANC
($110,000 in 1987 and $105,000 in 1988), as do numerous Scan-
dinavian and European charities. A West German student group
raised nearly $400,000 for ANC education projects in 1986. Jesse
Jackson's Rainbow Coalition pledged $10,000 in 1986; other U.S.
and European political groups have also promised financial support.[35] In 1985 and 1986 hundreds of Western political, business
and academic leaders made the pilgrimage to Lusaka and held
"discussions" with the leadership of the ANC. Those treks seem to
be diminishing in number, but the ANC's Western international
recognition and support seems to be growing rather than waning.

The East

The ANC may only receive "acknowledgment" from the
United States or recognition and some financial aid from other
Western nations, but it can count on very real recognition and
material support from the Soviet Union and its allies. Addressing
the MPLA-Labor Congress in Luanda, Angola, Joe Slovo of the
ANC and SACP stated,

> Botha and his U.S. allies would like to separate the ANC
> from its warm, fraternal relationship with the socialist com-
> munity, particularly with the USSR, a relationship which has
> been forged over many decades of unstinting and uncondi-
> tional assistance to our struggling people.[36]

The "unstinting and unconditional assistance" may be rhetorical vocabulary aimed for certain ears, but the Soviet bloc's past support of the ANC goes far beyond rhetoric. In late 1986 Oliver Tambo held what he described as an "historical meeting" with General Secretary Mikhail Gorbachev. In an interview with a British reporter, Tambo said, "We discussed forms of diplomatic support and material assistance and training for our cadres. Material assistance must include, wherever possible, the supply of weaponry to us."[37] According to sources within the ANC, 90 percent of the weaponry in the ANC arsenal is surplus Warsaw Pact material. "A limited amount of up-to-date equipment is provided by the Soviet Union."[38] The Soviet Union and its allies also supply instruction on how to operate weaponry ranging from rocket-propelled grenades to anti-tank guns. Former ANC guerrillas have described advanced instruction courses in guerrilla tactics and weaponry held in countries such as East Germany, Algeria and the Soviet Union.

In the past two years Moscow has grown more realistic and essentially cautious in its policies toward sub-Saharan Africa, including its relationship with the ANC. The Soviets still clearly view the ANC as the primary force in the anti-apartheid movement, but their recent statements seem to encourage the ANC to adopt more moderate strategies and tactics. Moscow appears to be shifting its emphasis in favor of a negotiated settlement rather than focusing on military options. (For further assessments of the ANC-USSR relationship, see chapter four.)

Regional

The Organization of African Unity (OAU) annually condemns the racist regime in Pretoria and calls on all of its members to support the national liberation movements. (Note the plural—the OAU has never explicitly stated that the ANC is the only liberation movement.) Virtually all of South Africa's neighbors, the "frontline states," recognize the ANC and offer varying degrees of support.

In March 1984 Mozambique and South Africa signed the Nkomati Accord that explicitly called for both countries to cease support and assistance to respective guerrilla movements. (South Africa had been aiding Renamo, a guerrilla movement aimed at overthrowing the Maputo regime, and Mozambique had been

giving haven to ANC guerrillas.) Mozambican President Joaquim
Chissano, emulating his predecessor Samora Machel, makes
regular statements expressing his sympathy with the ANC but
denying that Mozambique is aiding the ANC insurgents. In April
1988 South Africa and Mozambique agreed to renew their commitment to the Nkomati Accord, which had been ignored in varying degrees by both parties. Zimbabwe, on the other hand, has
made no such official and public agreement with Pretoria. The
ANC certainly has the recognition of the government of Prime
Minister Robert Mugabe; how much material support is provided
is difficult to determine. (There is clearly one element within the
ANC—the hard-line Marxists—that looks upon Mugabe's relatively moderate economic policies with contempt. Hence there has
apparently been some friction between Harare and the ANC.) The
Mugabe government allows the ANC to operate within Zimbabwe
and might, upon occasion, supply it with logistical support and
assistance.

Zambia hosts the ANC's official headquarters, and the Kaunda
government appears to have frequent and influential contacts with
the ANC leadership. Zambia is not financially capable of supplying the ANC with major assistance, but it does lend diplomatic and
non-military support.

Angola and Tanzania have both contributed to the ANC by
allowing it to have military bases within their borders. By mid-
1989, however, the ANC had to abandon the camps in Angola as
part of the Angolan-Namibian Tripartite Agreement. The ANC
appears to be shifting most of its bases to Tanzania and possibly
Uganda. Botswana, Lesotho and Swaziland take a much more
cautious approach, dictated by their economic and geographic
links to South Africa. (Lesotho expelled many ANC members after
it experienced a coup in 1985. In recent months, however,
Botswana seems to have become a frequent transit route for ANC
cadres coming into South Africa.)

The United Nations

In 1974 the General Assembly of the United Nations passed a
resolution giving recognition to "the national liberation movements as the authentic representatives of the South African
people."[39] It is interesting to note that the U.N. explicitly states
"liberation movements"—reflecting the understanding that there

is more than one legitimate revolutionary group. (The U.N. does not want to write off the black consciousness movements—AZAPO and PAC.) The ANC officially has U.N. observer status, which allows it to participate in General Assembly and Security Council discussions and debates when South Africa or southern Africa is on the agenda. Beyond the U.N. headquarters in New York, the ANC reaps international rewards via the worldwide network of U.N. Information Offices which distribute copies of the Freedom Charter and other information about the ANC. Financially the United Nations supports the ANC through education funds such as the U.N. Development Program. This program assists the ANC's Solomon Manhlangu Freedom College in Tanzania, as well as conferences and refugee programs which, directly or indirectly, promote ANC programs and initiatives.

In other multinational forums, the ANC has started to establish its "international credentials." The revolutionary group signed Protocol 1 of the Geneva Convention which pledges to abide by the international rules of war as a combatant in a war of liberation.[40]

Internationally, the ANC is gaining "acknowledgment" and "recognition" as well as financial and material support. The foundation for this assistance still rests with the Soviet Union and the Eastern bloc, yet clearly some in Europe, Japan and North America appear to be increasingly interested in contributing to the ANC's "legitimate authority" status. Certainly the ANC has international support which seems to be growing, but what about internal support? The ANC has been in exile for more than 25 years. Can it justly claim to be black (and white) South Africa's legitimate revolutionary authority?

Internal Support

When the ANC was banned in 1960, it counted approximately 100,000 South Africans as paid-up members.[41] If it were unbanned today, would that number be about the same, double or even tenfold? Measuring a revolutionary movement's internal support is far more difficult than analyzing the governmental and private sector assistance it receives from the outside world. The ANC's support, or lack of it, must be assessed via the assistance it receives from other extra-parliamentary groups, as well as the populace at large. This requires an examination of inter-group support and rivalries, as well as analysis of public opinion polls and other relative measuring devices.

ANC Sustainers

In a speech at the 75th anniversary of the ANC, President Oliver Tambo said,

> We have succeeded to create mass democratic organizations representative of the conscious and active masses, ranging from street committees to COSATU, to the UDF, and their affiliates and other democratic formations.[42]

The ANC has a host of supportive organizations, both legal and banned, in South Africa. Some of these groups represent small membership lists, while others claim a broad spectrum of support. Each of these groups promotes the goals of the ANC in its own manner and degree.

The political group that is the most closely associated with the ANC is the South African Communist Party (SACP). Oliver Tambo described the SACP's support of the ANC in this manner:

> Ours is not merely a paper alliance, created at conference tables and formalized through signing of documents and representing only an agreement of leaders. Our alliance is a living organization that has grown out of struggle.[43]

Alfred Nzo, Secretary-General of the ANC, explained the SACP's advocacy of the ANC in this light:

> ... both the ANC and the SACP are emerging as defiant standard-bearers marching at the head of the militant formations of the democratic movement ... the banners of our two organizations constantly flutter defiantly at the head of the revolutionary columns, proclaiming the imminent demise of the hated and dying apartheid system.[44]

In theory, the SACP-ANC alliance is complete and secure, at least until the first stage of the revolution has been completed. How that relationship might develop in a post-revolution South Africa is a matter of interesting speculation. Currently, however, the SACP's support for the ANC is unquestionable. Alfred Nzo concluded his speech to the 65th Anniversary of the SACP in London in July 1986 with a revolutionary battle cry: "Long live the South

African Communist Party! Long live the anti-fascist alliance between the ANC and the SACP "[45]

The United Democratic Front (UDF) does not have as concrete an alliance with the ANC as the SACP, nor does it so completely and unconditionally support the ANC. This is not to suggest, however, that the UDF does not cooperate with the ANC. Professor Tom Lodge suggests, "There is a great deal of admiration of the ANC by UDF leaders. If the ANC were to be legalized, the UDF would certainly be absorbed into the ANC."[46]

The UDF adheres to the Freedom Charter and in that respect is advocating and supporting ANC goals and intentions. In an interesting twist, however, the supposedly "less radical" UDF can, in fact, hold more radical interpretations of revolutionary policy. Tom Lodge explained,

> Elements within the UDF frequently interpret the Freedom Charter in a far more radical fashion than the ANC. They (UDF) see "private enterprise" as being limited to boutiques and small shops. Monopoly capitalism applies to anything larger than a shoe shine store.[47]

Nevertheless, the UDF often acts essentially as the legal spokesman for the banned ANC and in that respect represents a major supporting group.

The largest labor union, COSATU, has adopted the Freedom Charter and recognized the ANC as the lead organization in the national liberation movement. COSATU represents a broad range of trade unions with varied political and economic orientations; hence there is no monolithic support of any revolutionary strategy. The ANC, however, views COSATU's role in the revolution as particularly important, and recent developments in May 1987 demonstrated COSATU's ability to play a more radical and, therefore, supportive function for the ANC.

Providing a supreme political irony is another key group which qualifies as an internal supporter for the ANC—the South African government. It strengthens the ANC via political propaganda, suggesting the ANC has far greater political and military power than it actually possesses. The "total onslaught" mentality of the South African government gives the ANC prominence that it probably does not deserve. John Kane-Berman of the Institute on Race Relations writes,

The (South African) government has played directly into
the hands of the ANC by attempting to blame it for the current
violence (early 1986). The ANC is unquestionably doing all
it can to capitalize on the turmoil, but to suggest that it is the
main cause is to credit it with a logistical capability it doesn't
deserve to have.[48]

The SACP, UDF and COSATU represent extra-parliamentary
associations that, in varying degrees, support the ANC. The
SACP's support, relatively small and illegal, does not constitute
any great popular or grassroots assistance; its significance comes
in the form of influencing and shaping the ANC leadership and its
revolutionary strategies and tactics. The UDF and COSATU are
significant contributors to the ANC's legitimacy because they, in
fact, represent a relatively broad coalition of South Africans,
claiming numbers well into the millions. The leadership of the
UDF and COSATU definitely have strong sympathies toward the
ANC; how thorough the support for the ANC is within the UDF
and the COSATU rank and file is difficult to assess.

Internal Opposition

AZAPO

When asked about black opposition to the ANC, Solly Smith,
the ANC's Chief Representative in London, responded, "Well, the
ANC is the expression of the people—all other groups like AZAPO
are splinter groups. The ANC remains the will of the people."[49]

Perhaps Mr. Smith has been out of the country too long, but
"splinter groups" are frequently flexing their muscles within South
Africa and demonstrating their very determined opposition to the
ANC. South African newspapers and periodicals carry headlines
such as "Wararas vs. Zim Zims in Township," marking the very
real and devastating fighting between AZAPO-related groups and
those who support the ANC-UDF. (The Wararas are a nickname
for charterists—those who adhere to the Freedom Charter—and
the Zim Zims are in the AZAPO fold.) Nomavenda Mathiane, a
black journalist in Soweto, writes, "The fight between the two
(ANC and AZAPO) is wreaking more devastation than the fight
with the apartheid system."[50] In an editorial in the liberal monthly
Frontline, the editors assess the ANC-UDF-AZAPO conflict as
follows:

The war between AZAPO and the UDF is a civil war in the most classic sense. It makes enemies of people who have shared schools and churches and soccer teams and ties of blood and marriage. It poisons the community in which it exists. . . .[51]

In December 1986 pamphlets printed on UDF letterhead called for a mass mobilization "of all our fighting units" to destroy "the reactionary and racist AZAPO."[52] AZAPO has made similar pleas to its cadres and, as a result, hundreds of black South Africans have been victims of this undeniable conflict.

The strife between the two political organizations has its roots in the historical split between the ANC and the black consciousness movement in the early 1960s. Current perceptions, however, have sharpened the conflict between the ANC and AZAPO. Nomavenda Mathiane explains,

For AZAPO, the image of an ANC/UDF "ruler" is an image of Stalinist programs against dissidents, such as themselves. And for the ANC-UDF, whose eminence in the media bears a questionable relationship to its solidity in the townships, the idea of the wild men of AZAPO holding sway is no less terrifying.[53]

The AZAPO-ANC clash is a substantial hindrance to the ANC claim of representing "the people" of South Africa. The conflict, particularly in urban areas, will most likely continue and possibly worsen in the future.

Inkatha

Another key organization that clearly stands in the ANC's path of claiming "sole legitimate authority" is Inkatha. Oliver Tambo recognizes Buthelezi and Inkatha's clear stance against the ANC: "Buthelezi, encouraged to join the forces of the struggle, has instead emerged on the side of the enemy against the people."[54]

The ANC-Inkatha conflict first emerged in 1980. Prior to that year, Buthelezi and the ANC cooperated on various levels. Buthelezi himself had been active in the ANC Youth League at Fort Hare University. Albert Luthuli, one of the ANC's senior statesman in the 1950s and 1960s, was a mentor and advisor to the young Gatsha. Chief Buthelezi and Nelson Mandela of the ANC continue to correspond to this day, and Buthelezi is beginning to claim that the true spirit of the ANC and its early leadership is now being passed to him and Inkatha. He views the ANC in exile as having betrayed the true purpose and goals of the nationalist movement. The split between Inkatha and the ANC came at a meeting in London in 1980. Oliver Tambo and other ANC leaders met with Buthelezi in an attempt to extract from him a guarantee that ANC guerrillas would be given protection and assistance as they traveled through KwaZulu. (In 1980, many ANC guerrillas used Mozambique, which borders on parts on KwaZulu, as a launching pad.) Chief Buthelezi would not (and could not) make such a guarantee; the severing of ties between the ANC and Inkatha became complete and the relationship between them has become extremely hostile. ANC-UDF members frequently clash with Inkatha rank and file, particularly in the Durban area, but also in urban centers such as Soweto.

The cycle of violence between Inkatha and the ANC-UDF seems to be self-perpetuating. Accusations inevitably turn into bloody conflict which in turn results in retaliation. In late 1987 and early 1988 the Inkatha-UDF conflict reached a height around the Natal city of Pietermaritzburg where hundreds of people were killed in an often grotesque and chilling manner.

Some analysts suggest that the ANC-Inkatha conflict finds its roots in ethnicity—with the ANC being predominantly Xhosa and Inkatha representing the Zulus. Interestingly both organizations vehemently deny such a tribal explanation, yet it is difficult to ignore cultural histories and realities. Whatever the cause, Inkatha remains a stalwart against the ANC—from both a public support point of view as well as from a military perspective. The conflict between the two organizations is deep enough, both ideologically and ethnically. However, in mid-1989, the UDF and Inkatha began negotiations to end the violence in Kwa Zulu. These discussions were successful enough to encourage larger talks that dealt with broader issues between the UDF and Inkatha. A possible meeting between the ANC, COSATU, UDF and Inkatha may now be in the making.

The ANC enjoys a great deal of support from a variety of organizations, both legal and banned, within South Africa. The South African Communist Party, the United Democratic Front and various trade unions all support, in varying degrees, the goals and sometimes the means of the ANC. On the other hand, there are very real obstacles to a unified support of the ANC emanating from groups such as AZAPO and Inkatha. These extra-parliamentary organizations are critical in assessing the revolutionary elite's authority; but how do individual South Africans, both white and black, perceive the ANC? Is there support, antagonism or indifference?

ANC Support: How Broad, How Deep?

"The people are talking ANC, the government is talking ANC, everybody is talking ANC." A prominent black newspaper editor goes on to explain that "the ANC is the only group that has shown itself to be actively fighting the government, and it is respected for that. . . ."[55] Individual black and white leaders in South Africa span a wide spectrum of perceptions of the ANC. From total support to recognition to acknowledgment to accusations of charlatanism, the ANC evokes many responses.

Black and white religious leaders differ significantly in the degree of support they are willing to provide the ANC. At his enthronement ceremony when he became the Anglican Bishop of Johannesburg, Desmond Tutu stated, "We will not have peace until we have justice, and how can we have justice without the participation of the premier black liberation group, the ANC?"[56] Calling on the ANC to be one of the "participants" is only recognizing the ANC as an active player; describing them as "the premier black liberation group" is a significant endorsement.

The South African Catholic Bishops Conference met with the ANC leadership in Lusaka in April 1986. One result of that meeting was a message that Archbishop Denis Hurley sent to President P.W. Botha.

> We told him (Botha) that the internal and external extra-parliamentary opposition movements, like the UDF and the ANC, have a formula for South African unity and democracy in a non-racial state based on one person-one vote.[57]

Archbishop Hurley clearly assesses the ANC and its goals as legitimate and deserving of recognition.

Religious leaders, however, are not the only South African citizens who have met with the ANC and advocate recognition. Business leaders such as Gavin Relly, chairman of the Anglo American Corporation, and Tony Bloom, former president of Premier Group, have also made the trek to Lusaka. Such meetings are certainly not tantamount to support of the ANC, but they do express a very real recognition. John Chettle, former North American director of the business organization known as the South Africa Foundation, views the ANC in this light:

> It is a body which is obviously supported by a significant section of black opinion in South Africa. It cannot easily be left out of negotiations for a future constitutional frame-work in South Africa, although not until it ends its commitment to violence.[58]

But what are the attitudes of the man-in-the-street towards the ANC, particularly within the black community? One black journalist recently wrote, "If there was one man-one vote today, most people would vote for Botha—they are sick of these politicals causing trouble."[59] Hyperbole no doubt, but it reflects the desire of many, probably the majority of black South Africans, to get on with their education, jobs and raising a family. Turning their country upside down via revolution just does not seem to be a popular alternative to the current situation. When a black worker in Durban was asked if he belonged to Inkatha or any other political organization he responded, "I don't belong to Inkatha and I don't belong to the UDF or the ANC. I belong to my family and my church."[60]

This nonpolitical, or even apolitical, attitude seems to be evident within urban and rural areas throughout all of South Africa's provinces and "homelands." Yet the ANC seems to have made strides in recent years in getting more blacks involved in its movement, particularly among urban youth. The unrest and violence that became commonplace throughout the country in 1985 and 1986 certainly benefited the ANC's standing within the townships. Most analysts agree that the ANC cannot claim credit for initiating the massive unrest that led to P.W. Botha's State of Emergency in 1986, but the predominant anti-government feelings within the townships cannot but increase ANC recruitment and its general standing in the eyes of the black public.

The 1984 to 1986 nationwide violence was often locally inspired and controlled, with little coordination or logistical support from the ANC or any of its internal support organizations. Prior to the June 1986 State of Emergency, the bloody conflicts between black youth and South African police and defense forces, as well as between rival black organizations, escalated in a particularly frightful crescendo. What has come to be termed the "Khmer Rouge Factor" was beginning to set in. The "Khmer Rouge" were young "comrades" who adopted the concept of purging all of society (like their counterparts by the same name in Cambodia in the late 1970s). Anarchy became the goal, indiscriminate violence the means, a "reign of terror" at the very outset of "the revolution" strategy. Clearly in these instances the ANC had no control over these young radicals. In addition to the "Khmer Rouge factor," there was a growing wave of criminality that would pose as political protest. The borderline became very difficult to define.

The ANC attempted to tap the unrest for its own gain. ANC symbols such as its official flag and its songs were prevalent throughout many of the townships, yet few ANC officials would claim that they exercised control over the vast majority of the activities. Ken Owen, political analyst and an editor for *Business Day*, when asked if the ANC had been effective in tapping the unrest for its own gain during the 1984 to 1985 period, concluded,

> The ANC tries, but they are so ineffective and have such rotten and amateurish leadership that "the revolution" will happen without them. It happened in 1976 (Soweto) and again in 1985 to 1986. They sort of plug in on the end of it and grab the international credit. They don't claim to have control over the situation inside the townships, and they don't.[61]

The ANC's lack of control over various guerrilla actions was brought to light late in 1985 when an Amanzimtoti supermarket was attacked. Oliver Tambo, in January 1986, denied ordering the attack on the supermarket, but did not exclude the possibility that the attack was carried out by ANC insurgents acting without orders.[62] The apparent lack of control or authority over the civil disobedience, the political demonstrations and the violence certainly does not contribute to the ANC's "legitimate" claim. The violence of 1985 to 1986 does represent a powerful underlying discontent with the current racist system, but it does not necessarily imply support for the ANC.

Since the implementation of the State of Emergency in June 1986, with its drastic curtailment of individual liberties and freedoms, the violence in the urban centers has subsided. The "calm" might be attributed to a disillusionment that "the revolution" was not just around the corner. Tom Lodge suggested that "the danger of the ANC at present is that very aroused expectations of people in the townships may be followed by disappointment and apathy."[63]

Another possible explanation for the calm might be that the townships are taking a long-needed gasp—a brief relaxation before the next sprint. Whatever the reason, the ANC seems not to be on the minds and lips of South Africans as it was in 1985 and 1986. During those turbulent months streets and school buildings were renamed by paint brush in honor of leaders of the ANC. That excitement, however, seems to have waned. An Alexandra (township) schoolteacher explained in April 1987,

> The mood has changed. Before in a history class a student might stand up and demand, "Tell us about Mandela!" Many students boycotted classes. That has changed. The radical youth leadership is gone. . . . [64]

Whatever the current mood might be within the black community, it is evident that as the struggle continues, and it undoubtedly will, the ANC will need to show that it is more than just a revolutionary elite in exile. It would have to produce tangible results for the black (and white) populace to recognize and support it as a legitimate authority. The ANC's credibility will rest upon its ability to organize internal grassroots support. One way that popular support might grow is through increased guerrilla activities. The ANC clearly attracts support from the black population, particularly the urban youth, when it can demonstrate its military effectiveness against the government.

Archbishop Denis Hurley has suggested,

> Their (the ANC's) legacy rests with the fact that they were sending in guerrillas into the country on sabotage and attack missions and this gave blacks the conviction that the liberation movement was alive and active. [65]

The question the ANC must ask itself is how far guerrilla or revolutionary violence should extend. Should it include more "soft targets" that kill and maim both black and white civilians? When do guerrilla tactics begin alienating the very people that the ANC is attempting to attract? (This policy decision will be further examined in chapter four.)

In 1985 the late Percy Quboza, editor of the *City Press*, stated, "The reality that all of us must accept is that the ANC is the strongest black organization in South Africa. Their popularity runs

at around 80 percent."[66] Quboza' s suggestion of "80 percent"
opens the discussion of public opinion polls and the quantification
of the ANC's internal support. Very few polls have achieved an
authentic measurement of support for the ANC. (This is due to
certain intimidation factors by both the government and revolutionary elements and black perceptions of poll-takers.)
According to the U.S. Secretary of State's Advisory Council,
". . .at best 40 percent of black South Africans support Nelson
Mandela and the ANC. . ." or other organizations, such as the UDF,
that subscribe to the Freedom Charter.[67] A poll conducted by a
British firm attempted to measure support of "violence" in achieving a more just system. More than 63 percent of South African
blacks, according to the poll, believed that "violence is not justified"; 28 percent felt that it was justified. (Eighty-eight percent
of the whites felt it was not justified, versus nine percent who
thought it was.)[68] This is a clear rejection of the ANC's violent
tactics, but is it a sign of disapproval of the ANC itself? Another
poll conducted in 1986 confirmed that three out of four South
African blacks prefer "negotiations to violence."[69]

Polls are helpful guides in assisting measurement of support,
and therefore legitimacy in a nation that denies the most efficient
measurement: free elections. Opinion polls, however, do not always accurately reflect supporter resistance to a revolutionary
group's tactics, strategies and goals, much less the organization
itself. The definite rejection of the ANC's violent tactics, and the
overwhelming percentage of South Africans, both black and white,
who prefer negotiation to violence, does not bode well for increased support for the ANC's revolutionary strategies.

Perhaps this public antipathy towards a violent solution has
encouraged the ANC to search for non-violent approaches. In late
1988 and 1989 the ANC began to piece together strategies on
negotiations. Recently, the ANC has begun to examine preconditions for negotiations with Pretoria. Surely this more pragmatic
and non-violent course does not suit all of the ANC leadership
(particularly those like Chris Hani in the MK). But it appears that
the "negotiators" are, for the moment, carrying the day.

One final observation on the ANC's internal support focuses
on the difficulty any revolution might have when its elite is in exile.
Many of the ANC's top leaders have not been inside South Africa
for 20 or 25 years. Even a good portion of the "younger" leader-

ship—the "Soweto generation" which left South Africa after the Soweto riots in 1976—has not been back in more than 10 years. Former ANC members have described how the revolutionary elite in exile crave "common information" about South African society: they want to know if a new shopping mall is where the old brick factory used to be and what downtown Johannesburg looks like today.[70]

A university professor portrayed the ANC's lack of information in this manner:

> A colleague of mine flew up to Lusaka in December 1986 to meet with the ANC. She got on the airplane with a Sunday paper. When she arrived, they were pleased to see her, but extremely anxious to see the paper. They had seen their last South African paper two or three weeks earlier. Their news about South Africa is old. Imagine, if you will, the possibility of the U.S. being managed by someone who had not been in the U.S. for two decades.[71]

In a speech marking the 25th anniversary of the Umkhonto we Sizwe, Oliver Tambo identified this isolation.

> We (the older generation) had left our country in the belief that, when we come back with our martial skills, we would be received by our leaders occupying the front trenches and guiding us to battle. And now we were faced with the imponderable prospect of being cut off from the lifeblood of our revolution—our people.[72]

Being cut off from the people of South Africa creates a difficult hurdle for the ANC as it pursues its quest of "legitimate authority."

In summary, the ANC, one of two nationalist movements calling for armed revolution, has emerged as the leading candidate for authentic revolutionary leadership. In the eyes of the international community, the ANC is either (1)"acknowledged," (2) "recognized" or (3) financially supported. The West tends to acknowledge and recognize the ANC, while some European governments actually financially assist the revolutionary elite. The bulk of the ANC's military support comes from the Soviet bloc, but Moscow's approach towards military solutions appears to be changing.

Internally the ANC can look to the SACP, the UDF and COSATU for varying degrees of assistance. The other declared revolutionary movement, AZAPO, clearly views the ANC with great antagonism and exists as both a political and military challenge. Inkatha, the largest legal black organization in South Africa, also represents a difficult roadblock for the ANC claim of "sole legitimate authority." Tribalism, although apparently on the decline in urban areas, remains a problem for the ANC, as it is sometimes perceived as a predominantly Xhosa organization.

The ANC's apparent lack of control of the violence in the townships and its inability to harness the recurring discontent within the black population raises questions about its leadership and influence. The fact that it is an exiled revolutionary elite, cut off from its people, also poses problems for the legitimate-authority claim. Perhaps the most accurate assessment of the ANC's legitimacy is to describe it as one of a nucleus of organizations which clearly represents a large portion of the people in South Africa.

Though the ANC ought not to be seen as the sole heir to revolutionary leadership in South Africa, it does derive some authority from internal and external support. This support makes the ANC a key player in shaping the future of South Africa. How the ANC plays that role will determine whether this partial legitimacy is enhanced or diminished.

Four

Revolution with Right Intentions

However wonderful the first days of freedom were, no one in his right mind would march into the wilderness without the hope of a 'good land' on the other side.[1]

—Michael Walzer

The third criterion that a revolution must face concerns its goals. What is the revolutionary elite's vision for the future? How will the revolutionaries govern if they come to power? What are their intentions?

When analyzing a revolutionary movement's aspirations and goals, a purely objective assessment is nearly impossible, and perhaps not terribly useful. The revolutionary elite's vision for the future must be measured by some standard. In this book "the standard" utilized is that rooted in a distinctly democratic, liberal and Christian tradition, a tradition that pursues what St. Augustine called "*tranquillitas ordinis*," or the peace of public order.

To establish that a revolutionary elite considers its intentions to be good only begins the discussion, it does not end it. As one American political analyst wrote, "Good intention is not the same thing as intensity, for one could in his magnificent fervor be magnificently wrong."[2] Profound devotion to the revolutionary movement does not necessarily guarantee admirable goals.

In the current South African context, the revolutionary elite, the ANC, has expressed its vision for the future—its intentions—in a number of formulas. Like many 20th-century revolutionary movements, the ANC is frequently unclear about its ultimate goals. When asked what type of government the ANC envisions for South

Africa, Dumi Matabani, the ANC spokesman in the United States, responded,

> It is unfair for the ANC to be asked what type of government we will have. I don't want to count chickens before they hatch. The situation will decide what type of government we'll have.[3]

Nonetheless, the ANC has at times expressed its goals in more explicit terms. The published document known as the "Freedom Charter," first drafted in 1955, is frequently referred to by the ANC elite as an initial blueprint for the future. Building upon (and occasionally straying from) the Freedom Charter, the ANC has also demonstrated its intentions via various political strategies and alliances. Its 30 year commitment to an armed struggle, its allegiance to the South African Communist Party, its dependence upon the Soviet Union, and its recent commitment to a negotiated settlement all contribute to defining the ANC's ultimate intentions. The ANC's vision for the future is also influenced by its understanding of economics. And finally, its tactical approaches to fulfilling its visions often end up influencing (and possibly distorting) the vision itself.

The Freedom Charter

An ANC spokesman, Dumi Matabani, suggested that although the revolutionary group did not have a "blueprint" for the future, it did have some ideals toward which it was working. "We cannot say we are going to have this or that kind of government. Our Freedom Charter gives clues to what sort of government we are thinking of."[4] "Clues," hints, vague notions or whatever, the Freedom Charter is the primary written document that must be examined to glean the "official" intentions of the ANC.

In June 1955 a "Congress of the People" was held in Kliptown, near Johannesburg. The congress, convened by the ANC, the South African Indian Congress, the South African Coloured People's Organization and the Congress of Democrats, adopted the "Freedom Charter" which had been drafted some weeks earlier. The four sponsoring organizations declared their support for the charter, and it became their manifesto. (It is interesting to note that the initial purpose for writing the charter was as a pamphlet to attract support and interest for the Kliptown meeting.) The

Freedom Charter is a rather general document, relatively short in length, that broadly defines certain goals and ambitions. It begins,

> We, the People of South Africa, declare for all our country
> and the world to know that South Africa belongs to all who
> live in it, black and white, and that no government can justly
> claim authority unless it is based on the will of all the people.

Declaring that the "people shall govern" and that "all shall be equal before the law," the document seems to be firmly rooted in post-Enlightenment, Western, democratic traditions. The "economic section," however, begins to show signs of certain goals which can be associated with centrally-planned economies. The ANC itself describes the two economic clauses "as the very core of the revolutionary programme."[5] The clauses read:"The people shall share in the country's wealth," and "The land shall be shared among those who work it."[6] An ANC publication, *Colonialism of a Special Type,* interprets these ideas to mean "the seizure of economic assets, presently owned and controlled either by individual capitalists or capitalist companies drawn from the white minority or transnational corporations."[7]

Historically great political documents have been produced by men and women, known and unknown, who have had a very definite and distinct understanding of a political, economic and social order. Identifying the authors of the Freedom Charter, however, is a somewhat difficult task in that only one of the drafters has identified himself—the Chairman of the South African Communist Party, Mr. Joe Slovo. In its 1987 report to the U.S. Congress, the State Department wrote,

> SACP members played a significant role in drafting the
> Freedom Charter, which dovetailed with the party's
> longstanding strategy of promoting African liberation as the
> prerequisite to advancing the socialist cause.[8]

In addition to Joe Slovo, it has been suggested that Rusty Bernstein and Michael Harmel, both members of the SACP, lent an influential hand in authoring the charter.[9]

In a speech in London in 1986, Joe Slovo described the role he saw the Freedom Charter play in the revolutionary process: "The main thrust and content of the immediate struggle continues to revolve around the Freedom Charter, which provides a minimum platform for uniting all classes. . . ."[10] One cannot help but ponder what Slovo is envisioning when he uses terms such as "minimal platform." This, of course, leads to the problem of interpretation of any revolutionary document.

According to Tom Lodge, adherence to the Freedom Charter is nearly monolithic; virtually all ANC recruits can recite most of the charter by heart. But interpretation of the document reveals different perspectives within the ANC elite. Lodge points out that "for some in the ANC, the Freedom Charter quite nicely accommodates a broad African socialism."[11] It is also difficult to measure the exact constitutional implications of the document, especially since the ANC elite has not officially held up any constitutional form as a guideline. Lodge suggests,

> Leaders within the ANC, on various occasions, have made it quite clear that they don't have much admiration for American forms of democracy. But when they go to the United States they say the reverse. It is very difficult to tell. It is interesting to note that they are not particularly critical of Soviet democracy.[12]

Obviously the SACP element within the ANC elite has a clearly Marxist-Leninist interpretation of the Freedom Charter. But how influential and widespread is the one-party state vision among the ANC membership? Tom Lodge assesses the influence as follows:

> The most popular perception of the Freedom Charter with the (ANC) members would envision the kind of socialism that would have a dominant, strong central political organization which might accommodate within it different tendencies and ideas, but it would not tolerate a multi-party system.[13]

(This analysis differs from official ANC position supporting "multi-party, non-racial democracy.")

The Freedom Charter, the ANC's lodestar, prompts different visions for different people. How the outside world interprets the charter is important. Critical, though, is how the ANC elite perceives its primary document. For the SACP members the document is minimal, representing the first stage in a two-stage revolution that will conclude with a classless, one-party state. For others within the ANC elite the charter appears to be the guiding document that will guarantee political freedom and social justice within a socialist economic structure. To judge which interpretation represents the "true" perception is nearly impossible. That both of these visions exist within the revolutionary elite, however, is vital in assessing the ANC's goals.

Political Strategies

If the Freedom Charter represents an overarching statement of goals and aspirations, then certain political strategies and alliances are the means to achieve those goals. Four such strategies will be briefly examined: (1) The ANC's position on negotiations; (2) its attitude towards armed struggle; (3) the ANC-SACP alliance; and (4) the ANC's relationship with the Soviet Union. All four of these strategies or alliances are seen as working towards the fulfillment of the visions of the Freedom Charter. Yet, as in all revolutionary struggles, the political means influence the very goals the revolutionaries are pursuing.

Negotiations

During an interview in Washington, D.C., in August 1986, Dumi Matabani, the ANC's North American spokesman, said, "It is unfair for us to be pushed to negotiations. . . . I am not saying we don't want negotiations, but we are not begging for negotiations."[14] Oliver Tambo has emphasized, "Our target is not negotiations; it is the end of the apartheid system."[15] The ANC's Radio Freedom broadcast from Addis Ababa stated: "We are not fighting for the opportunity to reach the negotiating table. We are fighting to seize power. . . ."[16]

Past conditions for negotiations enunciated by the ANC were simple: "Coming to the (negotiating) table would not be for anything else than to discuss the mechanics of handing over power to the victorious masses led by their vanguard movement."[17] In the past, the ANC has demanded "the disbanding of the South African Defence Force before it will consider talks."[18] In a Radio Freedom broadcast the ANC explained,

> The PFP (Progressive Federal Party) and its so-called liberal cohorts should not be blinded by the willingness and readiness of the ANC to go to the negotiating table into believing that we have suddenly abandoned the armed struggle and are pinning our hopes for liberation on a negotiated settlement. Instead it is the political and military victories on the ground, the stinging blows delivered by our heroic com-

batants . . . that are finally going to drive the apartheid rulers to the negotiating table."[19] This belligerent attitude no doubt still exists within certain elements of the ANC. But in recent years there has been a new tone emerging.

Since 1988 there has been an increasing interest in negotiations. From 1987-89 the ANC released a series of documents and articles describing official goals of negotiations as well as preconditions for negotiations. The ANC and Pretoria seem to be approaching that pre-negotiating stage of "talks about talks." This is a far more fluid situation than in the mid 1980s. It appears that the ANC will continue the twin-track approach of pursuing certain types of negotiations, while at the same time, continuing the "armed struggle." This dual strategy will, in time, probably lead to some sort of internal strategic decision between the "negotiators" and the "warriors."

'The People's War'

During his Washington, D.C. visit in early 1987, in which he met with Secretary of State George Shultz, Oliver Tambo quite plainly suggested, "I can think of no condition in which we (ANC) would call the armed struggle off. . . ."[20] The ANC has been committed to armed revolution since 1961, with the concept of a "people's war" becoming the rhetorical banner since the early 1980s. At the 25th anniversary of the Umkhonto we Sizwe (Spear of the Nation—the ANC's military wing), Tambo explained,

> The actions of Umkhonto we Sizwe on a sustained basis and the continuous upsurge of the masses . . . showed that our bases would, of necessity, have to be located among our people. Along this path our theory and practice of revolutionary warfare came to be properly understood in terms of people's war.[21]

The commitment to revolutionary warfare has not always been the policy of the ANC. Albert Luthuli and other influential members of the early ANC attempted to avoid armed struggle and to pursue the ANC's initial objectives without the use of force. Mrs. Albert Luthuli recently stated, "Like my husband, I am sick and tired of violence. Albert worked towards a better South Africa by negotiation, not by the barrel of the gun, which the ANC of today is doing. It makes me very sad indeed."[22] The ANC's commitment to negotiations often seems secondary at best, as Johnny Makatini, the ANC's former representative at the United Nations testified. Displaying his willingness for the "sacrifice" of millions of his countrymen, Mr. Makatini once commented, "If there were only four million of us left after the revolution, that would be better than the present situation."[23]

By the late 1970s the strategy of revolutionary warfare had been fully adopted by the ANC leadership. Those within the ANC who had been the prime motivators behind the strategy of a "people's war" had apparently won. But after the 1984-1986 violence, and perhaps more importantly, after the USSR's new interest in "political" solutions, it now seems as if many within the ANC are reassessing the "people's war" strategy. There are, no doubt, still many within the leadership that see the armed struggle as the only vehicle for a victory over apartheid.

The South African Communist Party

The goals and aspirations of the SACP are similar to the ANC but go beyond them as well. The SACP is committed to the Freedom Charter, the destruction of apartheid, and—what distinguishes them from ANC "nationalists"—the formation of a "classless, one-party state." Writing in the *African Communist,* Joe Slovo, Chairman of the SACP, explained, "The Communist Party (SACP) pledges its unqualified support for the Freedom Charter. It considers that the achievement of its aims will answer the pressing and immediate needs of our country along non-capitalist lines to a communist and socialist future."[24]

The SACP envisions a future South Africa which is a Marxist, one-party state. In formulating its final aspirations, the SACP has come to rely heavily upon, not surprisingly, Marxist analysis. During the 60th anniversary of the SACP in London in 1986, Joe Slovo suggested that the oppression of blacks in South Africa was not a result of racism, but simply "the result of the class warfare inevitable in any capitalistic economic structure."[25]

The SACP's analysis of South Africa has, for the past 15 years, centered upon an holistic vision of the political economy. That is, all distressing features of the South African society—racism, inequality, poverty—are repeatedly attributed to "capitalism."[26] At an ANC Youth Conference in Tanzania, Moses Mabhida, a member of the ANC's National Executive Committee commented, "The ANC will head the struggle for a democratic revolution. . .while the Party (SACP) will be responsible for leading the advance to socialism."[27]

The theory of a two-stage revolution clearly remains the primary strategy within the SACP elite. The Central Committee of the SACP foresees the ANC leading the first stage, the "nationalist phase," and then the Communist Party will be at the forefront of the vanguard that ushers in the second stage, which will culminate in a communist society. (There are differing revolutionary theories and goals within the SACP. Moses Mabhida, for instance, suggests that "The Party does not contemplate a neat progression from one stage to another." He proposes, rather, that it would be preferable if the party can thoroughly destroy South Africa's political institutions "during the struggle for the seizure of power during the first stage." If such a destruction of the existing political order can be accomplished in the first stage, then "the advent of another 'October' phase of the Revolution might not be necessary.")[28]

The SACP's goals and strategies are straightforward: Revolutionary warfare will produce a two-stage revolution which will ultimately usher in a class-less, communist society. A critical issue at hand is the depth and breadth of the relationship between the SACP and the ANC, and perhaps more importantly, the explicit and implicit influence the SACP has upon the ANC's own goals and strategies.

In a speech to the SACP in London in 1986, Joe Slovo said,

> The alliance between the Communist Party and the ANC has no secret clauses. . . . The historically evolved connection between capitalist exploitation and racist domination in South Africa creates a natural link between national liberation and social emancipation, a link which it is virtually too late to unravel.[29]

There has been extensive speculation on the number of the ANC's 30-member National Executive Committee which are SACP members. In 1986 the CIA placed the number at 18; other reports have estimated it from 14 to 15.[30] The exact number is not nearly as important as the general attitudes and perceptions the ANC elite has towards the SACP. Former SACP and ANC members have shed some light on the alliance and the dynamics that occur between the two revolutionary organizations. In a 1982 hearing before the U.S. Senate Judiciary Committee, Mr. Bar-

tholomew Hlapane, formerly a member of the ANC's National
Executive Committee and SACP's Central Committee, explained,

> No major decision could be taken by the ANC without the
> concurrence and approval of the Central Committee of the
> SACP. Most major developments were, in fact, initiated by
> the Central Committee.[31]

(After his testimony, Mr. Hlapane returned to South Africa
where he was assassinated in December 1982.)

Perhaps the SACP's clearest influence upon the ANC is
through the Umkhonto we Sizwe (MK), the Spear of the Nation.
Joe Slovo was the primary promoter, organizer and leader behind
the development of the MK. Slovo and other SACP leaders apparently maintain firm control of the Spear of the Nation and
continue to advocate its crucial role in the revolutionary movement. (In late April 1987 it was announced in Lusaka that Joe Slovo
had stepped down as the official Chief of Staff of the MK.)[32]

Perhaps the most central aspect of the relationship is the
adoption by the ANC leadership of a way of thinking, a Marxist
method of assessing, analyzing and interpreting goals and intentions, and it was the SACP which brought to the alliance a distinc-
tively Marxist analytical approach. Tom Lodge explains the
situation in this light,

> Certainly not all members of the ANC are members of the
> Communist Party. But I think it is the case that a popular
> rhetoric used by most ANC members has Marxism in it. Most
> ANC members are committed to adhering to Marxist prin-
> ciples. Their Marxist rhetoric is stronger and means more
> than, for instance, what took place in Zimbabwe. ANC mem-
> bers have a strong understanding that 'the struggle' is both a
> racial struggle and a struggle between capital and labor; this
> understanding goes beyond just rhetoric.[33]

The goals and visions of the ANC have been influenced by
Marxist analysis, promoted chiefly by the SACP members within
the ANC elite. The rather general vision portrayed by the Freedom
Charter clearly shows signs of its authors' socialist preferences;
the ANC's somewhat nonspecific goals are often colored by Marxist analysis. In contrast, the SACP has clear, explicit intentions
and visions for the future of South Africa—a two-stage revolution
which will culminate in a classless, one-party state.

The Soviet influence

The late 1980s has been a period of transition for the ANC-USSR relationship. With glasnost, perestroika, Soviet budget demands and the South African State of Emergency all acting as influential factors, Moscow appears to be reassessing its analysis of the South African situation as well as its relationship with the ANC. In March 1989, Boris A. Asoyan, deputy chief of the Department of African Countries in the Foreign Ministry stated that, "In our opinion, we doubt that revolution in South Africa is possible, if you're talking of revolutionaries storming Pretoria."[34]

As early as August 1987, Gorbachev said "The collapse of apartheid is inevitable. But we are not supporters of the thesis that the worse things get the better it is."[35] The leadership within the ANC's military wing might find such statements troubling, particularly when they focus directly upon military strategies. In the March 1989 interview, Mr. Asoyan implied that the Kremlin might want to consider scaling down their military support of the ANC. "Too many arms," he suggested, "are concentrated in the poorer areas of the world and not just conventional arms, but quite sophisticated weaponry."[36]

The foundation for this new Soviet approach seems to be grounded in an awareness that the end of apartheid will come through political dialogue rather than military action. Yuri Yukatov, head of the Soviet Foreign Ministry's Department of African Countries, said, "We would prefer a political settlement and want apartheid to be dealt with by political means. Any solution through military means will be short lived."[37] The explanations for this shift in Soviet thinking are many. Dr. Winrich Kuhne, a German scholar specializing in African affairs, writes,

> The most important reason for the shift in emphasis from armed struggle to a political solution has little to do with what is happening in South Africa.
> It is a matter of global politics. Leaders in the Kremlin are concerned that an uncontrolled escalation of violence in South Africa would interfere with their much higher-ranking interest in continuing a dialogue with Washington and other Western countries on arms control, economic cooperation and other matters.[38]

Although Moscow seems to be redefining its relationship with the ANC, it remains the Congress' primary international supporter.

Boris Asoyan clearly states that "We support the ANC and we regard it as the mainforce in contemporary political life in South Africa."[39] But the Kremlin appears to be applying pressures upon the ANC that moderate some of their military tactics (particularly bombing of civilian targets) and encourages political rather than military solutions.

Some Soviet Africanists have attempted to outline the political process leading to a post-apartheid South Africa. In late 1986 at a "Conference of Peace, Cooperation and Social Progress," Mr. Gleb Starushenko suggested three proposals for the revolutionary movement and its goals for South Africa: (1)the revolution should adopt a program that "does not envisage a broad nationalization of capital property as an indispensable condition"; (2) the ANC might work out comprehensive guarantees for the white population which could be implemented after the elimination of the apartheid regime; (3) the ANC should consider the "idea of a parliament— one formed on the basis of proportional representation, and the other possessing the right to veto on the basis of equal representation for all four major racial communities."[40]

Moscow's motivation for a more compromising strategy for the ANC is also linked to Soviet economic interests. Dr. P.R. Nel, Director of the Institute for Soviet Studies at the University of Stellenbosch, suggests, "The Soviets' ideological requirements may in bilateral relations play second-fiddle to tangible commercial interests."[41]

Currently, Moscow has certain agreements with South African companies, specifically within the mineral sector. Nel has commented that the Soviets' interest in South Africa's strategic and commercial minerals "would not necessarily imply that the USSR wants exclusive control over South Africa's minerals. There is no hard evidence that Soviet strategy planners consider this a realistic goal."[42] In fact, Nel implies that the Soviets are quite comfortable with their existing arrangements with the South African mineral companies and that Moscow's "current lucrative commercial arrangement is secure—something that might not be possible under a strong-willed black government which will be pressed to nationalize most resources."[43]

As the USSR-ANC association continues to change, Winnie Mandela's now infamous statement calling the Soviet Union "the torchbearer for all our hopes and aspirations"[44] takes on new meaning. The Moscow influence on the ANC at present is shaped more by moderation and glasnost, than by hard line Stalinist attitudes.

Economic Visions

"The transfer of power to the people must therefore be accompanied by the democratization of the control and direction of the economy so that indeed the people share in the wealth of our country."[45] The "sharing of wealth," according to Oliver Tambo's above interpretation, raises the question of nationalization or expropriation of South Africa's existing land and capital. How many and which industries or corporations might be targeted to be nationalized by an ANC government is an open-ended question. Clearly there are some in the ANC elite who, as Tom Lodge observed, would nationalize everything larger than a barber shop. Others in the ANC discuss economic goals in less specific, more ambiguous terms, such as "sharing the wealth" and "economic justice." It is interesting to note that those in the ANC who appear to devote time to economic questions tend to be the more Marxist-oriented leaders.

Joe Slovo, in a 1986 speech in London, said,

A victory will bring the immediate need to begin directing the economy in the interests of the people. This must obviously involve immediate state measures on the land question and against giant monopoly complexes which dominate mining, banking, and industry.[46]

When Slovo speaks of the "giant monopoly complexes" he is referring to South Africa's "big five"; that is, Anglo American, Barlow Rand, Old Mutual, Rembrandt Group and Sanlam. But for many of the ANC "economists," the vision is not complete if only these large corporations are nationalized or expropriated. Slovo, for instance, envisions a temporary "mixed economy, controlled to assist the well-being of the people." This "mixed economy" stage will "facilitate the continuing drive towards a socialist future."[47]

According to a report that summarizes a meeting between the ANC and National Union of South African Students (NUSAS), the "ANC advocates an anti-monopoly democracy in which monopolies are nationalized." According to the same report, the ANC considers 75 percent of the shares on the Johannesburg Stock

Exchange as representing "monopolies."[48] On the land question,
the ANC writes, "To redress historic injustice, the national liberation movement is required to seize the land from its present owners
and restore it to the dispossessed and exploited black tillers."[49]

Dumi Matabani of the ANC explained in Washington, D.C. that
"we will have to nationalize white farms." The decision of which
farms will be taken over by the new government would "be based
on output, the amount and size of farm."[50]

In the case of land, it appears that the ANC's goals of
nationalization or expropriation would focus on the larger, more
productive tracts. The nationalization and expropriation tools have
become somewhat controversial within the ANC elite. Solly
Smith, the former ANC chief representative in London, for instance, takes a more cautious approach to the redistribution of
wealth.

> We (ANC) know that resources have to be used different-
> ly, that there has to be a redistribution of wealth. This does not
> mean nationalization instantly. . . . What it does mean is a
> realistic assessment of the economic structures and the way
> these need to be changed.[51]

The ANC's rhetorical expressions concerning redistribution of
wealth must be separated from its actual intentions and goals.
Depending on the audience, the ANC's leaders might stress
strategies of expropriation, while at other times they diminish the
significance of a centrally-controlled economy, and speak of pursuing "a mixed economy."

Professor Tom Lodge separates the ANC's rhetoric from its
ultimate intentions by using Zimbabwe as an example: "In comparison to the rhetoric of Robert Mugabe, the ANC is much more
committed to its socialist rhetoric, and will implement it to a
greater degree than did Mugabe."[52]

Lodge suggests that, unlike South Africa, Zimbabwe did not
have an industrial base that included trade unions.

> Mugabe was never confronted with demands for ex-
> propriation by organized labor. In the South African context,
> however, extra parliamentary groups, including the unions,
> define themselves by advocating expropriation and
> nationalization. It will be expected and demanded.[53]

It is important to recognize the significant pressure groups outside of the ANC elite which attempt to shape the revolutionary movement's economic goals. Elijah Barayi, President of COSATU, for instance, has stated,

> This country (South Africa) is in a crisis because of capitalism; if we at least nationalize the big firms, then the government could look after its people and the people could look after the government. I believe COSATU is a socialist organization and I would like to see a socialist state in South Africa.[54]

In 1988 the ANC published a set of constitutional proposals that have come to be known as the "Lusaka Amendments." The intention of the proposals was not to supersede or replace the Freedom Charter, rather it claims to be an attempt to translate the broad charter into some kind of constitutional framework. The ANC has defined the proposals as "guidelines."

Unfortunately, even these "clarifying" proposals still speak in vague terms, particularly on the structuring of the economy. One encouraging note is that the specific commitment of the Freedom Charter to nationalize the mines, the banks and "monopoly industry" is not included. At the same time the "Lusaka Amendments" declare that "the State shall have the right to determine the general context in which economic life takes place" and the private sector "shall be obliged to cooperate with the State in realizing the objectives of the Freedom Charter."[55]

With these proposals, the ANC has attempted to flesh out its economic policies. Nonetheless, discussion of economic issues remains generalized and at times confused. Tom Lodge suggests that the ANC must be careful not to alienate different constituencies with specific economic pronouncements.

> Presumably the ANC uses a different language when it talks to visiting South African trade union delegations from the terminology employed, say, when encountering a deputation from NAFCOC (the Black Chamber of Commerce).[56]

Lodge has concluded, however, that the Lusaka Amendments' "economic guidelines would, if implemented, require a quite radical redistribution of productive property."[57]

Whether the ANC would follow an economic path similar to the Marxist-oriented FRELIMO regime in Mozambique, or more on the order of Mugabe in Zimbabwe, is a matter for speculation.

Currently it appears that the ANC elite does not have an experienced international economist such as Mugabe has in Bernard Chidzero. (Chidzero is Zimbabwe's Minister of Finance and a former executive with the International Monetary Fund.) Exactly how the ANC will fulfill their vision of "sharing South Africa's wealth" remains to be seen.

The ANC's Tactics

Benito Mussolini's pre-war motto was "Action! Deeds! These alone matter. Leave the theory to scribblers!" There is a strong element within every revolutionary movement which has little time for theoretical goals and ultimate visions; they instead are preoccupied with bringing the revolution to birth, making it happen. From smuggling in ammunition clips for AK-47s, to planting limpet mines near nuclear reactors, the "realists" of the ANC might not hold discussions on the nuances of economic policy, but over time they play a very significant role in defining the revolutionary movement's goals.

The principle of proportionality, one of the two main principles of the *jus in bello,* is not one of the five criteria pertaining to the "*ad bellum*" theory for initiating revolution. As the revolutionary climate within South Africa continues to escalate, however, the tactics and methods already employed by the ANC must be assessed as proportionate or disproportionate to its objectives. In particular, the way in which the day-to-day workings of the Congress may influence its visions and goals for the future must be brought into focus.

It appears that a certain segment of the ANC leadership remains committed to armed struggle. This commitment has manifested itself in an escalation of force in the past 10 years. Large oil storage tanks were blown up in 1980; plastic explosives did limited damage to a nuclear reactor in 1982; and in 1983 the ANC appeared to abandon its "military only" targeting and began a campaign of violence that included "soft targets." In May 1983 a car bomb in downtown Pretoria killed 19 and wounded 200. In a May 1986 Radio Freedom broadcast, the ANC's tactics were defined.

Let us take all our weapons, both rudimentary and sophisticated, our necklaces, our grenades, our machine guns, our

AK-47s, our limpet mines and everything else we can get—let us fight the vigilantes, together with the apartheid regime, together with the police and the army.[58]

Between April 1985 and April 1986 there were 193 "serious acts of terrorism" attributed to the ANC.[59] (Since late 1988, however, there has been a significant slowing in terrorist acts against civilian targets.) Not long after the Pretoria bomb blast in 1983, Oliver Tambo stated,

> We have avoided civilian casualties because we don't think that individual people are to blame for apartheid. But it's an armed struggle—it's bound to develop into quite a war and the civilian population will be affected.[60]

In a Radio Freedom broadcast in 1985, the ANC declared,

> The battlefield has been confined to the areas we, the oppressed black people, live in. The whites of this country now have to be rudely awakened from the dreamland that they have closed themselves into.[61]

The township violence of 1985 and 1986 further escalated the use of various violent tactics in the name of "armed struggle." "Necklacing" became a daily event, where a "collaborator" or "traitor" was doused with kerosene, had a similarly soaked tire placed around his or her neck and was set ablaze to die a terrifying death. Throughout late 1985 and early 1986 the ANC elite performed a rhetorical dance around the necklacing issue; never outwardly condemning it, nor ever actively promoting it. As the young comrades in the townships began to rely heavily upon this tactic, the ANC realized it would lose significant support if it denounced "the necklace." By August 1986, ANC Secretary General Alfred Nzo, in London, stated, "Whatever the people decide to use to eliminate those enemy elements is their decision. If they decide to use necklacing, we support it."[62]

In this instance the revolutionary elite was clearly influenced by the radical activists on the ground. The ANC leadership in Lusaka felt it had no choice but to adopt the tactics of the radicals in the townships. "Street justice," with its "people's committees" and executions by necklacing, is a strategy that belies an ANC committed to democracy and rule of law.

Are the car bombs, the necklacing and the massive intimidation of the black community appropriate to the specific ends they

are meant to achieve? Since early 1988 the ANC itself has seemed
to question these tactics. The Congress's elite, however, are caught
within a tactical dilemma. They need to continue the "people's
war," including its violent black-on-black dimension, because it
demonstrates to the South African people, both black and white,
that the ANC is a vibrant movement which can influence events
and make a difference. The down side to the soft-target strategy,
however, is that many South African blacks are becoming alienated
by the very violence that is suppose to impress them. The answer
for many in the ANC elite is a combination of two tactics: armed
struggle and "mass mobilization." According to Solly Smith, of the
ANC, mass mobilization will usher in the revolution and destroy
the existing system. In order for a general mobilization to occur,
he identifies three requirements: alternative education (that is,
"liberation education"); unity with the workers via the trade
unions; and political education. These are the building blocks to a
successful mass mobilization.[63]

Exactly how the ANC plans to install nationwide "alternative
education" is not clear. But it is evident that forms of revolutionary
rhetoric are being actively used in some black schools. Cooperation with the unions is already underway and appears to be growing
with various labor union-ANC "dialogues" and meetings. "Political education" is difficult to define but appears to focus on explain-
ing the ANC's goals for a post-apartheid South Africa. This would
include the ANC's already significant public relations strategy in
Europe and the United States.

The mass mobilization strategy has, of course, worked suc-
cessfully in other political scenarios around the world. Further
examination of the likelihood of a successful mass insurrection
will be explored in chapter six. The exact relationship between the
advocates of a "people's war" and the supporters of "mobilization"
is unclear. There are many within the ANC, represented primarily
by the Umkhonto we Sizwe, that remain committed to an armed
revolution, using violent tactics that include, and often stress, soft
targets. For these revolutionaries, mass mobilization is a tactic that
is useful only in that it promotes general destabilization, allowing
the MK to gain military ground.

Discerning a revolutionary movement's ultimate intentions is
a difficult task that requires not only an evaluation of official
rhetoric, but also the various internal pressures that exist within

any revolutionary elite. The Freedom Charter remains the ANC's general manifesto and statement of purpose. This single, general document does not stand alone, however, in defining the ANC's visions for the future. The "Lusaka Amendments" of 1988, the Congress' shifting attitudes towards negotiations, its fluid relationship with the Soviet Union and the failure to effectively use the 1984-1986 disorder all point to the necessity of the ANC rethinking many of its policies and strategies. It is a promising omen when ANC leaders begin to use language such as "multi-party democracy" when they describe their vision for a post-apartheid society. But their promises of "justice and freedom" must be balanced with the recent history of the ANC giving its blessing to "people's committees" that handed down "sentences" including necklacing.

From a democratic, liberal, Christian point of reference, the ANC's goals and intentions are not completely reassuring. Its vision for the future, which in the past has been shaped by revolutionary strategies and tactics, does not seem to guarantee a democracy that would defend justice and freedom for its citizenry. Yet its renewed interest in negotiations, and its specific rhetoric centered around "multi-party democracy," bodes well for a post-apartheid South Africa.

In the mid 1980s, an ANC leader was presented with a hypothetical scenario that described a free and fair election with universal suffrage which resulted in the ANC receiving 40 percent of the vote. What would the ANC do with that type of election outcome? The answer: The revolution would continue, for the true will of the people had not been expressed.[64] It is apparent that for some leaders in the ANC, "democratic politics" means only politics in which the ANC rules. The "justice now—freedom later" rhetoric carries some very large caveats that we must heed. The more recnet clarification on the ANC's view of "multiparty democracy," however, does not easily fit with the above scenario.

The ANC elite has produced a set of goals which are a rather sophisticated blend of nationalism and Marxism. The strategies and tactics used to achieve those visions have in the past been far less sophisticated and at times blatantly ruthless. The intentions that the ANC holds for the future of South Africa have changed, just as the organization itself has since its founding in 1912. Perhaps the ANC is rethinking its overtly Marxist statements and principles of the 1960s, 70s and 80s. Perhaps the glasnost of Moscow is being reflected in the Congress' vision of tomorrow's South Africa. Perhaps the failed strategies of the "people's war" will be replaced by the pragmatic understanding of political negotiations. The old visions of the ANC should not be endorsed because they may well lead to a society which is consistently more oppressive than the one that currently exists. Our hope is that new visions that are truly committed to multi-party democracy with individual freedoms and liberties will develop and supplant the totalitarian goals of past decades.

Five

Revolution as a Last Resort

*A people have a right to rise up in violence to overthrow
a tyrannical or utterly corrupt government if all channels
for peaceful redress of grievances have been closed to them
and there is no prospect of opening them.*

—Abraham Lincoln

A revolution is justified, according to this fourth criterion, when all reasonable means of peaceful settlement have been exhausted. Implicit in this criterion is the belief that a revolution is not an end in itself—that revolutionary violence is only a means to an end, as discussed in the last chapter outlining "right intentions." Within neo-Marxist revolutionary theory, however, the concept of "last resort" has been totally shunned. In fact, according to Marxist theory, the revolution should be the first, not last, avenue; violent revolution should be the initial choice. "The violent act of revolution itself is therapeutic; only by this degree of self-assertion against the exploiter does the proletarian become aware of who he is and what he may become."[1] The "self-actualization" or "conscientization" that an armed revolution supposedly provides the oppressed becomes the goal; the concept of a "last resort" holds no place in Marxist revolutionary theory.

This chapter will examine whether the ANC has explored all nonviolent channels for change and whether the people of South Africa perceive that all peaceful avenues have been exhausted. One method of determining if all choices other than armed revolt have been attempted is to examine what, if any, changes have occurred in the society due to nonviolent pressure. South Africa has experienced a diverse mixture of economic and other pressures that have produced significant alterations in the apartheid structure. In the recent past a pattern seems to be emerging within Afrikanerdom which no longer suggests a monolithic Afrikaner mindset incapable of ever retreating from its people's privileged position in society.

The ANC: Pushed to the Last Resort?

The ANC is quick to claim that it attempted to pursue "peaceful strategies" for nearly 50 years, and, because of the violence of the apartheid system, was forced to adopt armed struggle as its last resort. In recent years the "systemic" violence theory has grown in popularity among the ANC elite. This rationale suggests that "the system" initiated the cycle of violence, and the ANC is only responding to the initial violence of the state.

There have been numerous analyses of this official ANC position, including one by the Reverend Robert Robertson of Johannesburg, a prominent member in the End Conscription Campaign. He has suggested that the ANC's nonviolent years were considerably shorter than the half-century regularly claimed by the Lusaka elite.

> The ANC actually only attempted nonviolent tactics for eight years, 1952 to 1960. Previous to 1952 they spoke of nonviolent tactics but never partook in nonviolent actions. It was in 1952, during the Defiance Campaign, that the ANC first offered nonviolent resistance.[2]

Perhaps Reverend Robertson's argument rests on semantics, but the historical account is important. Contrary to popular claims, it does not appear that the ANC had an active nonviolent resistance campaign for 50 years. Ken Owen, an editor of *Business Day* in Johannesburg, describes the ANC's rhetoric of exhausting all peaceful channels in this manner:

> The ANC did not try everything possible before it resorted to armed struggle. It went to violence because its most active and leading members were closely allied with the SACP and they chose to go to violence because they believe in revolution.[3]

Mr. Owen's assessment appears to fit historically since the ANC elite was heavily influenced by the SACP members, particularly beginning in the late 1950s and early 1960s. And the

Marxist revolutionary theory to which the SACP adheres visualizes the revolution not as a "last resort," but the first and only choice.

Perhaps more important than the implicit explanations for why the ANC turned to violence is the problem that the ANC embraced armed revolution at the very time in which authentic reform, via nonviolence, had its greatest chance of success. Nadine Gordimer, a South African novelist, has described South Africa in the 1980s as "a society in the midst of howling change." Can the ANC's total abandonment of peaceful change within this rapidly altering society be justified?

The Black Community and Violence

In numerous public opinion surveys the South African black population has demonstrated its reluctance to adopt violent solutions. In December 1986 a poll conducted by Omnicheck showed that 75 percent of the black population preferred negotiations to violence.[4] Nonetheless, there are many within the black community that have fully embraced the violent solution. Many more, however, in Helen Suzman's words, "long for a peaceful solution." Suzman, for years the liberal stalwart of the anti-apartheid campaign within Parliament, suggests "There is a great middle ground of blacks who are not totally politicized and radical. There are still many blacks I would call moderate, prepared to go along with a shared society on a non-racial basis. Among those I would count Nelson Mandela; I would not be too sure about the rest of the ANC."[5]

Many leaders in South Africa, both black and white, have described "the middle ground" as representing the place where the majority of South Africans are today. There is no doubt that polarization of the nation increases every year. On the far Left the radicalization of black urban youth continues. And on the Right the radical militarization within the Afrikaner community also grows. But, as Dr. Oscar Dhlomo, Minister of Education for KwaZulu, states, "The middle ground still represents by far the majority of people in South Africa."[6]

The ANC claims that it pursued all possible peaceful roads to effect change, and all of those avenues were blocked. The black (and white) communities in South Africa clearly do not accept such a claim, and hold on to the expectation that peace, justice and freedom can be accomplished without looking down the barrel of a gun.

The Other Options

If South Africa is not going to accept armed revolution as the "last resort," what can the "middle ground" offer that will effect genuine change? What has worked in the past? Nonviolent strategies have had their greatest impact in the 1980s. Apartheid is cracking, and radical change is within grasp. The change within Afrikanerdom is critical to this possibility—this will be examined shortly. The other crucial elements rest with economic developments and the cultivation of racial goodwill.

On the economic front the key is the interdependence between the white and black communities. The South African economy is firmly based on interdependence, and as the balance of economic power continues to shift towards the black community, its economic leverage will continue to increase. Using this economic leverage is one of the primary nonviolent strategies that the "middle ground" has embraced. So far the economic strategy for spurring change has been by far the most effective conduit for reform. Dr. Merle Lipton, an economist, sees a pattern of white South Africans showing a willingness to compromise when their racial prejudice damages their economic interests. If they cannot pass on the cost of apartheid to somebody else, they retreat from apartheid.[7]

Black economic clout continues to grow through a number of vehicles, including the trade unions, consumer purchasing power, black-owned companies, black management in publicly held corporations and recently acquired land ownership rights. Recent economic studies have shown that black South Africans account for nearly 50 percent of the Gross Domestic Produce (GDP) and therefore hold tremendous purchasing power.[8] This consumer power has been effectively used as an instrument of change, as was demonstrated by successful consumer boycotts in Port Alfred in 1985 and Port Elizabeth in 1986. Port Alfred, a small, conservative town in the Eastern Cape, had a two-week consumer boycott which prompted white business leaders to pressure the town council into meeting certain demands. As a result of the boycott, troops were withdrawn from the township, and black leaders took over the management of the local health clinic and other social services. Economic tools have been far more effective in bringing authentic reform to South Africa than has the ANC's attempt to foster a "people's war." Sheena Duncan, former president of the Black Sash, put it succinctly: "The critical successes have been the consumer boycotts, rent boycotts and the work stayaways. They have been so successful that even the ANC has begun to recognize them."[9]

Chief Buthelezi has also recognized the role of economics in the reform process: "The upward mobility of blacks is generating far more potent political forces than the armed struggle can possibly do."[10] Buthelezi's antipathy toward the ANC aside, the economic power the black community is acquiring is becoming a very potent political force. The bargaining power of the trade unions, the purchasing power of the black consumer and the management power of black-owned businesses all contribute to the political leverage that South Africa's blacks are now beginning to experience.

Other nonviolent strategies and tactics have also contributed in pressuring Pretoria into authentic reform. Civil disobedience of various types and forms has begun to erode some of apartheid's basic pillars, such as the Group Areas Act and the Mixed-Marriages Act. When the churches and other groups financially supported an Indian family when it moved into Mayfair, a "white" suburb of Johannesburg, they were opting for a nonviolent mode that eventually resulted in the de facto collapse of Group Areas in that suburb. Likewise, when the churches simply ignored state laws prohibiting interracial marriages and clergymen married men and women across color lines, they were practicing a form of civil disobedience that eventually resulted in the repeal of the Mixed-Marriages Act.

All of these nonviolent attempts to effect significant change required an underlying expression of "goodwill" among all South Africans. "Goodwill," a rather overused and abused word in South African society today, represents reasonableness, a willingness to look at and discuss various options for society. This willingness is, for the first time, emerging in Afrikanerdom—and that will be discussed shortly. "Goodwill" persists within the black population, despite the abuse it has suffered. John Kane-Berman, president of the Institute on Race Relations, refers to this as the "eighth wonder of the world." After decades of being second-class citizens, denied political and economic rights, the majority of the black community is still willing to pursue a nonviolent, reasonable course that would end apartheid and introduce a non-racial, democratic South Africa. Eagerness for negotiations is the key manifestation of this black "goodwill." Such eagerness does exist—as is evidenced by the above-mentioned 1986 poll.

The Institute on Race Relations has, in the recent past, conducted research programs which examine negotiations that are taking place on various levels within South African society. John Kane-Berman explained,

> Our research has indicated that despite the publicly stated positions of some people and some organizations against negotiations, there has, in fact, been a fair amount taking place. People are much more willing to talk than you might believe reading the *New York Times*. Our 1985 survey concluded that there was a great deal of willingness to talk, and I suspect our 1986 review will produce similar results.[11]

Clearly the KwaZulu-Natal Indaba has gone a long way in demonstrating that negotiations are not only possible, but can also produce realistic results that have significant impact on the political, economic and social climate of South Africa (see chapter eight). The Indaba has encouraged other serious attempts at multiparty negotiations in both the Cape and the Transvaal, and it is hoped it will set the stage for numerous local and possibly national talks. "Goodwill" is alive and well within the South African black community, but to take it for granted is to push South African blacks closer to opting for the "final resort" of armed revolution. The South African government has done little to encourage this willingness to talk, and has, it appears, done much to inhibit and destroy the "goodwill" that remains. Perhaps the white community in South Africa, particularly Afrikanerdom, is now recognizing the net results of such disregard for the reasonableness found in the black community and is beginning to rethink many of the liabilities of being a privileged citizenry.

Cracks in the White Wall

The changes in Afrikanerdom are significant in relation to the fourth criterion of "last resort" for two critical reasons: it represents the overall "howling change" that has been sweeping South African society, and it gives increased substance to the belief that further radical reform can materialize and the "last resort" of armed revolution can be avoided. Frederick van Zyl Slabbert, former leader of the Progressive Federal Party (PFP), summarized the change in Afrikanerdom in sociological terms.

Afrikaners are now bourgeois, upper-middle class, the Babbitts of Bloemfontein. They are beginning to feel ashamed of their racism. Their tribal bonds are weakening. Afrikaner hegemony and solidarity are crumbling.[12]

The past decade, specifically the past five to six years, has shown a movement away from the Verwoerdian understanding of the political, economic and social interrelationship between blacks and whites in which apartheid is so firmly rooted. The primary supports of apartheid are being questioned and in some cases, being torn down. This is not to suggest that Afrikanerdom en masse is lurching to the Left. What is occurring, however, is a change within the Afrikaner elite. The principal mechanisms that make up and define "the white tribe of Africa" include: the Dutch Reformed Church, the academic-intellectual sector, the "cultural societies" such as the Broederbond, the expanding Afrikaner business sector and the political parties, particularly the National Party. In every one of these sectors that make up "Afrikanerdom," there have been recent divisions. The schisms have occurred because the traditional is being challenged, certain tenets are being revised and there is a backlash, a resistance to the change. Afrikanerdom is for the first time becoming fluid, as the white tribe enters into the late 20th century.

The Dutch Reformed Church (NGK), frequently referred to as the "National Party at prayer," is the largest white church in South Africa. In the past the NGK has been a strong supporter of apartheid principles and legislation. In October 1986, however, the church synod met in Cape Town and produced a remarkable reversal. The synod passed a resolution which clearly stated that apartheid cannot be biblically supported, a claim that the NGK had consistently made in the past. All of the "apartheid theology" that was developed in the 1950s, 1960s and 1970s, the explanations giving a theological and ethical justification for apartheid, were scrapped. The synod wrote,

> . . . the conviction has gradually grown that a forced separation (apartheid) and division of peoples cannot be considered a biblical imperative. The attempt to justify such an injunction as derived from the Bible, must be recognized as an error, and should be rejected. . . . The NGK is convinced that apartheid as a political and social system by which human dignity is adversely affected, and whereby one particular group is detrimentally suppressed by another, cannot be accepted as a Christian ethical principle because it contravenes the very essence of neighborly love and righteousness and inevitably that of human dignity of all involved.[13]

Professor Johan Heyns, occasionally referred to as the "exorcist of apartheid," was elected as moderator of the NGK in 1986 and has been one of the guiding forces behind the church's public rejection of apartheid. As chairman of the Department of Theology at the University of Pretoria and now moderator of the Dutch Reformed Church, Heyns is an integral member of the Afrikaner elite who is forcing his people to rethink the basic structure of apartheid. He has consistently challenged his people to think about their privileged position.

> Apartheid is neither logical, ethical, or justifiable. If the government proceeds with this form of apartheid, we (the church) would criticize it, because it is contrary to scripture. We have already made headway. We protested the policy of migrant labor, and it has ended. Such confrontation is the prophetic duty of the church.[14]

These radically reformed positions have their cost. In June 1987, a conservative "whites only" church was founded. Known as the Afrikaner Protestant Church, this splinter group affirms separation of the races on biblical grounds. Perhaps the very phenomenon of a schism within the church demonstrates that Professor Heyns and others are pursuing very real (and to some, very threatening) goals.

Three years after the Cape Town synod that stated apartheid could not be biblically supported, the Dutch Reformed Church took one more important step and pronounced apartheid a sin. The General Synodical Committee in March 1989 stated,

> We confess with humility and sorrow the participation of our church in the introduction and legitimation of the ideology of apartheid and the subsequent suffering of people. We declare that . . . the ideology of apartheid is a political and social system whereby human dignity is adversely affected, and whereby one particular ethnic group is detrimentally oppressed by another, it is therefore a sin.

Along with the church's realignment there has been a movement within academic institutions. In the months leading up to the May 1987 parliamentary elections, some 30 professors at the University of Stellenbosch—perhaps the citadel of Afrikaner higher education—publicly announced their decision to leave the National Party in response to the party's unacceptably slow pace of reform. Professors at other Afrikaner universities, such as Pretoria and Rand Afrikaans, followed suit. More than 300 university professors nationwide supported a statement that denounced the current pace of reform as far too slow. W.P. Esterhuyse, Professor of Philosophy at Stellenbosch, is one of the academicians who have been advocating a new approach. "Ultimately we need to change specific laws. But our job, particularly in the universities, is also to change attitudes and behavior."[15]

Changing Afrikaner attitudes and behavior begins by challenging the suppositions that currently make up the foundation of apartheid. At the Afrikaner universities those challenges are being vocalized and considered. Challenging the pillars of apartheid and destroying them are, of course, two very different acts. As Professor Sampie Terreblanche of Stellenbosch University is quick to point out, "Changing Afrikanerdom will be difficult. Three or four swallows don't make a summer."[16] Professor Esterhuyse, however, already detects the substantial beginnings of change in many Afrikaners' attitudes.

> People are not only yearning for new ideas. They also want a new political style. . . . Unhappiness with the NP and its leadership does not simply concern the pace of reform. It is concerned with the nature, the goals and strategies of reform itself.[17]

The Broederbond, or brotherhood, is a cultural organization, once rather secret in nature, whose *raison d' etre* is to sustain and preserve Afrikaner culture. Members of the Broederbond represent a wide diversity of talents and perspectives, from politics to educa-

tion, from business to the arts. In the past a highly conservative
organization, both in structure and policy, the Broederbond is
beginning to reflect a more enlightened attitude toward political,
economic and social questions. It has been reported that since the
early 1970s the organization has been searching for alternatives to
apartheid.[18] A "working document" produced in 1985 and circu-
lated among members stated, "The rights of all groups should be
advanced and fulfilled."[19]

Perhaps not revolutionary on the surface, the idea of "black
rights" being "fulfilled" is a considerable step for the Broederbond.
Broederbond chairman Jan Pieter do Lange explained, ". . .There
is a tremendous need for more contact (between the races) to build
up mutual understanding."[20] Other Afrikaner cultural organizations have sprung up, partially in response to the apparent
liberalization within the Broederbond. Many of these groups view
"black rights" as the precursor to the abandonment of Afrikaner
culture and ethnicity. The divisions within Afrikaner cultural
groups are intense and often hostile, reflecting how the "white
tribe" attempts to understand its future in Africa.

The Afrikaner business community, once small and inconse-
quential compared to the English industrial circles, is growing in
size and importance. Carl Mouton, who runs the largest Afrikaner
architectural firm in Natal, suggests, "The goal is power-sharing,
it is the only way to save me and my black brothers."[21] Mouton
was active in the Indaba process and is quick to endorse negotiations at all levels. The Afrikaner business associations, although
not as progressive or forceful as the English-speaking commercial
groups, are part of the changing Afrikaner elite.

A decade ago the National Party (NP) was not simply a political party in the American sense of the word; it was a "volk"
party—a party of the people, all of the Afrikaner people. It was, in
a sense, the political wing of Afrikanerdom. What the party said
and did had the backing of all of the other institutions within
Afrikanerdom: the churches, the universities, the cultural groups
and the farming and business organizations all lined up behind and
supported the NP. Like all institutions in Afrikanerdom, the National Party elite has been changing. With the challenges and
changes there have come splits; the monolithic Afrikaner political
party no longer exists. More than 40 percent of the Afrikaner
population now votes for the Conservative or HNP parties. (This

loss of support from within Afrikanerdom has been made up by the dramatic increase in English-speaking support for the NP.) What P.W. Botha hoped would never happen has happened; politically, Afrikanerdom is split. This fluidity within white South African politics bodes well for the future of democracy. No longer does an Afrikaner politician have to battle with the party, the church and the Broederbond. Now he can remain within the boundaries of Afrikanerdom and simply challenge the party platform, either from the Left or the Right.

But how has the recently developed political fluidity borne any positive results? Changes have occurred on both an attitudinal level as well as a practical one. Political attitudes can be measured on the rhetorical level, and the practical changes on a legislative plane. In September 1985 P.W. Botha gave a speech which held as its centerpiece the following ideas: "My government and I have made a choice and thereby I must stand or fall. It is a choice for constitutional, social and economic reform."[22]

Whether Mr. Botha is committed to his rhetoric and how he defines his terms, are key questions. But the fact that he is now thinking and speaking such language is a sign of movement. Few could imagine the heir of Verwoerd stating at the opening of Parliament in 1986, "We have outgrown the outdated colonial system of paternalism as well as the outdated concept of apartheid."[23] And, although he was forced later to retract his statement, Foreign Minister Pik Botha has suggested that someday South Africa would have a black president.

The National Party leaders' speeches and rhetoric do reflect a certain attitudinal shift, but how have they converted this new found "enlightenment" into political action? Professor Nic Olivier, PFP member of Parliament, commented,

> If someone had said to me seven or eight years ago that P.W. Botha would head a government that abolished Influx Control (pass laws), the Immorality Act, the Mixed-Marriages Act, allowed blacks to own land outside the homelands, legalized and liberalized black trade unions and talked about apartheid as an "outmoded concept," I would never have believed it.[24]

The National Party has other big hurdles to face in the future. The Group Areas Act and Population Registration legislation are

two of the final pillars of apartheid that must be pulled down. P.W.
Botha recently said,

> It is strange that we are prepared to travel in a car with a
> coloured and allow him to ride on our bakkie [truck]; but when
> he wants to live close to you, then there is trouble. We must
> try to keep our sense of proportion in this matter.[25]

Reform legislation, much of which has a significant impact on
the daily lives of all South Africans, has passed with little applause
from the outside world. The lack of a laudatory sentence or two is
perhaps understandable in that the paramount questions of constitutional reform and authentic political power-sharing have only
begun to be addressed. The constitutional reform of 1983 that
produced the Indian and coloured chambers in Parliament was a
rather benign beginning that did not confront the ultimate issue:
authentic black representation in Parliament. (It was, however, the
1983 constitutional change which helped precipitate the formation
of the UDF and laid the immediate groundwork for the 1984 to
1986 unrest.) Nevertheless, the international community has been
negligent in recognizing the significance of what has developed
within South Africa in the last eight years.

The May 1987 election resulted in the National Party maintaining firm control of Parliament. Particularly interesting about
the election was the large amount of support that the NP garnered
from the English-speaking population. For the first time the NP is
dependent upon the English vote to remain in power. Historically
more progressive than the Afrikaner population, the English supporters of the NP will most likely continue to pressure their
newfound party toward adopting a faster pace of reform. Since the
May 1987 election, the National Party continues to broadcast its
desire to begin "authentic negotiations." However, it has yet to
embrace the Indaba, or even grant Natal and KwaZulu permission
to conduct a referendum allowing the citizenry to decide. Botha
has appointed Stoffel van der Merwe to pursue negotiations on
"constitutional development." Van der Merwe has said that he will
approach a wide field of black leaders concerning future talks.

> The representatives will have to convince a suitable num-
> ber of their people on the ground. There is nothing to be
> reached by drawing a lot of puppets into it, because they won't
> be able to deliver the goods at the end of the day.[26]

Adding to the increasingly fluid political dimension of Afrikanerdom is the leadership change and the election in September 1989. President P.W. Botha's 11-year reign will come to an end, and with it a new generation of National Party politicians will move into leadership positions. National Education Minister F.W. de Klerk appears to be the most likely successor to President Botha. He became head of the National Party after Botha suffered a stroke in January 1989. After Botha announced that he was stepping down and elections were to be held, a number of key members of the State President's cabinet also announced their retirement. National Party leaders such as Chris Heunis, Minister for Constitutional Affairs, and Stoffel Botha, leader of the NP in Natal, will no longer be cabinet officials.

There has been a great deal of speculation on what Mr. de Klerk's policies might be and what kind of leadership he will provide. He is a man that is notably familiar and comfortable with the white South African political system. His father was a senator and his brother a popular journalist. As leader of the NP in the Transvaal, de Klerk has been known for his cautious approach toward reform. As Minister of National Education, he attempted to tie financial assistance for universities to their ability to restrain student unrest. But after de Klerk's election as the NP's national leader, he has made statements that contain hopeful signs. In a May 1989 speech to Parliament, de Klerk said,

> What is necessary is a real breakthrough towards a workable and just system offering fair opportunities, meaningful participation and security to all the people of this country...The NP believes that the solutions to South Africa's problems lie mainly in a single concept: justice for all.[27]

Whether Mr. de Klerk is fine tuning his rhetorical language for Western ears or truly desires to lead South Africa into a new dispensation is unknown. What does seem certain, however, is his commitment to the parliamentary system; a belief clearly not shared by his predecessor. De Klerk will most likely dismantle, or at least reduce, the non-parliamentary "securocrat" system that P.W. Botha had installed. The new president will rely more heavily upon the NP caucus (made up of NP Members of Parliament) and might even consider returning to a more Westminster style system with himself as Prime Minister rather than President.

Afrikaner politics has changed, and with it the opportunities for radical reformation have increased. The NP no longer dominates the Afrikaner voting public. It does, however, remain as the undeniable primary force within South African politics, thanks in large part to the English-speaking population. To the left of the NP, the former Progressive Federal, which lost its role as the official opposition party to the right-wing Conservative Party in 1987, has merged with two independent parties to create the new Democratic Party (DP). The Democratic Party is currently sorting out its leadership positions with former Ambassador to Great Britain Denis Worrall, former PFP head Zach de Beer and former Independent Party leader Wyand Molan as the triumvirate.

The rise of the CP as the official opposition party has clearly had its effect on the body politic. Resisting any significant reform, the CP has won a number of municipal elections which enabled it to reinstate apartheid laws that had been abolished or ignored. Many pundits believe the CP has peaked and its gains in the September 1989 elections will be minimal. The white right-wing backlash is difficult to measure, however, and if economic conditions worsen, the CP will likely make parliamentary gains.

The net result of this political fluidity is an opportunity to initiate new and meaningful reforms.

Has South Africa come to a point where there is no other solution than to grab a gun and begin an armed revolution? King Goodwill Zwelithini Ka Bhekuzulu of the Zulus has stated, "I believe that we have not yet reached a stage where I can call on my people to take up arms. That time may come, but this is not yet the time."[28]

The majority of blacks in South Africa remain hopeful that there are other avenues to take to alter the gross injustices of apartheid; armed revolution is not the only way out. Their hopefulness and faithfulness seems almost graceful to an outside world. There is no doubt, however, that the nation continues to spin toward greater polarization; yet "goodwill" still resides in most South Africans. The lack of enthusiasm and commitment to a violent solution, particularly on the part of the black community, not only points to the "goodwill" that remains, but it also suggests that black leaders inside South Africa must be witnessing developments and signs that give them encouragement for a democratic future.

Economic factors have played a major role in effecting positive change on all levels of society. The increase in black consumer power, trade union power and the expanding black managerial and ownership power all contribute to the relatively recent rise in political leverage the black community possesses. It is this nonviolent, economic leverage that blacks have used to gain their most significant political victories.

Negotiations such as the KwaZulu-Natal Indaba have also provided a hopeful alternative to armed revolution. The Indaba has spawned other negotiations in the Cape and the Transvaal, and it is hoped it will inspire authentic discussions on a national level.

One of the key ingredients in providing realistic, nonviolent alternatives is the ever-changing nature of Afrikanerdom. Harold Pakendorf, former editor of *Die Vaderland,* assessed "the white tribe" in 1987 in this manner: "There is a growing realization that something has to give. People are now saying when there is a change, not if."[29] The Afrikaner elites within the church, universities, cultural groups, business community and politics have all come to the realization that the special privilege guaranteed to them by apartheid must end.

The leaders of Afrikanerdom have changed course, but will the masses follow? For the man in the pew to hear that his church has radically changed its theology, for the farmer who sends his son to Stellenbosch to see him vote for the new Democratic Party or for the factory worker to witness his Afrikaner boss promote a black man over him is a cultural and often personal jolt. For the vast majority of Afrikaners the 1990s will be very confusing, full of change—for some threatening and for others exciting. Afrikanerdom is not only cracking, but it is also emerging. For the first time it is becoming immersed in enlightenment ideas and truly entering the democratic world. But if the radical polarization process continues to spin toward revolutionary violence, many South Africans may well react in fear and abandon their movement toward meaningful reform.

The ANC and others claim that all peaceful attempts at authentic change have been tried and failed, but the majority of South Africans, both black and white, appear to disagree. With the success of nonviolent strategies, particularly those based on black economic power, and the signs of a willingness to change within Afrikanerdom, it must be concluded that, at this time, all

reasonable means of peaceful settlement have not been exhausted.
The fourth criterion is not met.

Six

Reasonable Hope of Success

> *Or what king, going to encounter another king in war, will not sit down first and take counsel whether he is able with ten thousand to meet him who comes against him with twenty thousand?*

> —Luke 14:31

The fifth and final "ad bellum" criterion bypasses theory and hypothesis and brings reality to the fore: Does the armed revolution have a reasonable chance of succeeding? This question requires an examination of military and strategic factors, including the numbers of revolutionary soldiers, their training experience, their armaments and their internal and external support systems—all in comparison with the current regime's defense forces.

In evaluating how opposing military forces judge each other's "chance of success, " there is invariably an element of bias which must be taken into account. Twentieth-century revolutionary commanders are notorious for portraying complete victory as "right around the corner." On the other hand, commanding generals of the regime will often refuse to recognize the authentic possibility of revolutionary success. An objective, realistic assessment is mandatory if the criterion is to carry any significance. Within the South African context this fifth criterion has both obvious and subtle applications. The ANC elite has within it a small element which firmly believes an armed revolt is close to toppling the Pretoria regime. This optimistic view will be explored. There is, however, firm evidence revealing a very lopsided comparison between the South African Defense Forces (SADF) and the Umkhonto we Sizwe (MK). The trained armies' insurgency and counter-insurgency capabilities, as well as South Africa's unsuitability for guerrilla warfare will be examined. How South Africans themselves assess the likelihood of a revolutionary victory—however biased or ill-informed—is important for setting the psychological foundation for revolutionary success. This optimism, or skepticism, is key in measuring nonmilitary factors within this criteria, particularly the likelihood of what has come to be referred to as "mass mobilization." Recent international political scenarios have given rise to a new hope within some circles that South Africa's revolution will succeed via such a mass mobilization.

The Jericho Complex

Richard John Neuhaus has identified a frequent phenomenon within many revolutionary movements across the 20th-century globe: "The revolutionaries are possessed with the Jericho Complex, believing that the walls will collapse if only they shout loud enough."[1]

There is, in fact, an element within the ANC elite that Tom Lodge describes as "the military romantics." According to Lodge, "It certainly is not the dominant view, but there is a core of military romanticists or insurrection romanticists in the ANC that sees victory at hand."[2] The romantic military rhetoric has a number of sources and purposes. Clearly, as Lodge suggests, there is an element within the ANC elite that actually envisions a victory to be near. For other members in the Lusaka hierarchy, however, the "success rhetoric" is there to bolster the grassroots support. If the leaders do not portray success as near, they will not be able to recruit new followers.

In a speech marking the ANC's 75th anniversary, Oliver Tambo preached, "But the people's army, Umkhonto we Sizwe, must act boldly against the apartheid enemy, to reduce its strength, force it further into the defensive and prepare conditions when our superior forces will overrun and overthrow the regime of terror."[3]

Oliver Tambo, as seasoned a veteran as he is, most likely does not believe that the day the MK will "overrun and overthrow the regime" is near at hand. In one of his limited interviews, Joe Slovo, former head of the Umkhonto we Sizwe, explained to a Western journalist, "We (the ANC) are not going to destroy the regime just with sabotage blows, even if we managed to double or triple the scale of activities."[4] With the exception of the military romantics, the ANC elite understands the long-term nature of an armed revolution that faces a sophisticated and committed militia like the one the apartheid regime has developed within the last two decades. Although young ANC leaders such as Dumi Matabani pledge that the ANC "is prepared to dig the Afrikaners out,"[5] for the most part, they are fully aware of the dimensions of the task that awaits them.

SADF vs. Umkhonto we Sizwe

According to the U.S. Secretary of State's Advisory Committee on South Africa, "The South African Defense Forces (SADF)—army, navy, air force and medical corps—is the best trained and equipped military on the African continent."[6]

In 1988 the SADF consisted of 106,000 full time members: 64,000 conscripts and 42,000 permanent force volunteers. In addition to this highly trained force, there are 317,000 "citizen-force reservists." All of these reservists have had military training, and many have seen combat in Namibia or Angola. (All white males are required to serve in the armed forces or perform conscientious objector duty.) The defense budget in 1987 was more than R 5 billion (U.S. $2.5 billion) and was expected to increase in subsequent years. The R 5 billion military expenses represents only about four percent of the Gross National Product (GNP). A regime that is faced with an authentic revolutionary threat could easily raise military spending. (In comparison, the Soviet Union's military budget is estimated to be 14 percent of GNP; Israel's is 28 percent.)

The size of the Umkhonto we Sizwe is difficult to measure, as the ANC gives no official numbers. Estimates have ranged from 5,000 to 10,000 trained men. The number of these insurgents who actually operate inside South Africa is an even more elusive figure. A South African Embassy spokesman places the number of fully trained ANC operatives within South Africa's borders as "well under 100."[7] The CIA places its estimates closer to 2,000; the International Institute for Strategic Studies in London places the figure around 500.[8] Whatever the number, it is evident that these combatants have no secure territory in which to reside, rest, receive instructions, pick up armaments or otherwise operate. The revolutionaries are on the move, usually only remaining inside the country for relatively short periods of time.

Military logistics remain a critical hurdle for the MK within South African borders. Border infiltration is absolutely vital to the ANC's military success. There is no Ho Chi Minh Trail, and it doesn't appear likely that one will emerge. Natural land barriers, such as extremely harsh desert (in the northwest) and difficult mountain terrain (around much of Lesotho) limits accessibility to population centers that are needed for revolutionary militia support. Other border regions, particularly along much of the Botswana and Zimbabwe border, are inhabited primarily by white farmers who often work in close concert with the SADF, monitoring insurgency activities. Perhaps the most likely routes of support would be through Swaziland and southern Mozambique. Kruger National Park, on the Mozambique border, has its own hazards, but it is also relatively easy to patrol. Swaziland remains the most likely link to the outside, and it may become the primary conduit for supplying the revolutionary militia. (The Swazi government, however, is generally cooperative with the SADF.) By late 1987 and early 1988, the most active ANC border infiltration was via Botswana, near Gaborone.

It is important to note that the front-line states will undoubtedly pay a price for supporting and assisting the ANC's military objectives. SADF raids into these sovereign nations over the past 10 years may well be just a foreshadowing of what the future holds. One former SADF officer explained, "The army and air force won't fight the war inside South Africa; the front-line States will end up seeing the most action and destruction."[9]

Evidence that this reality is not lost upon the front-line State leaders is contained in the Nkomati Agreement with Mozambique, as well as the relatively restrained military support for the MK from nations other than Angola and, to a lesser extent, Tanzania.

The SADF-MK military statistical comparison is completely and utterly lopsided. If the ANC were to launch any form of guerrilla warfare beyond its present occasional bombings of military and civilian targets, the SADF would dominate and probably crush the effort. The SADF's manpower, its communication and transportation systems, its counter-insurgency actions (including its rather massive infiltration schemes) and its military hardware all pose a military obstacle that must be depressing for the ANC leadership. The 106,000-member armed forces, backed up with the 317,000 reservists, obviously out-matches the ANC's 500-2,000 insurgents within the borders. But what are the non-military aspects of a revolution's success? What is the nation's perception of an armed revolution's chances of success? Could there be some form of public insurgency on a national scale?

The National Psyche and Mass Mobilization

Beyers Naude, former General Secretary of the South African Council of Churches (SACC), articulates the way in which many South Africans assess the fifth criterion: "To create the impression that there could be any successful action to overthrow this government is, to my mind, an illusion."[10]

In 1984 Chief Buthelezi went as far as to place the unlikelihood of a successful revolution within a certain time frame.

> There is no way, no way at all, in which it is possible in the next fifteen to twenty years to envision any circumstances in which blacks could confront this government with violent force and have any hope of success.[11]

Representing many of the KwaZulu leaders, King Goodwill Zwelithini expressed his frustration, as well as realism, in assessing the military situation in 1986.

> I come from a stock of people who know how to fight for freedom. I would, however, be irresponsible to call on my people to take up arms in order to be mowed down by the South African Defense Forces—and to die futilely without us achieving our freedom. . . . As a descendant of warrior kings, I consider it childish to indulge in saber-rattling games with someone who is far better armed than you are.[12]

Derrick Thema, a black journalist living in Soweto, arrives at a conclusion which also echoes much of the black community's realism: "The SADF, the counter-insurgency actions, and the country's unsuitability to guerrilla warfare all militate against a full-scale revolution."[13] The national psyche, black and white, seems to harbor no illusions of a successful armed revolution in the near future. At the core of this society's perception is an understanding of what James Michener so accurately portrayed as "the covenant." There is a covenant, a commitment, that rests within the Afrikaner people to remain and live and thrive in the land that they believe God promised them. That land, that society might change and be reshaped, perhaps even radically, as Afrikanerdom continues to assess its privileged position. But it will change and evolve under the direction of Afrikaners. The larger mentality is only a mortar shot or limpet mine away; a "scorched earth" policy is not outside the realm of possibilities. Underlying the South African's understanding of why an armed revolution will not succeed is the hard reality that, if it ever did, there would be nothing left. Frank Martin, one of the Indaba's co-conveners, explained, "If there is anything close to a successful revolution, everybody will be the losers. Those that pick up the pieces and take power after such a bloodbath will inherit desert."[14]

Most South Africans have arrived at the conclusion that armed revolution has very little hope of success. But most South Africans, black and white, also do not want an armed revolution to succeed because it will mean the destruction, the violence, the race war that is too terrible to contemplate. Archbishop Denis Hurley said,

> A successful revolution would turn into a guerrilla war with attacks carried out by infiltrators. This such thing could be more than just cruel; it could lead to total destruction, devastation, collapse of this country."[15]

In *The War of the Flea,* Robert Taylor suggests that a revolutionary movement's aim "is not to win decisive and bloody battles in which government forces are beaten, but to create an intolerable situation for the occupying army.[16] If the ANC cannot win decisive military victories, could it at least effect a "mass mobilization" that would be relatively short-lived in bringing down the Pretoria regime? "People Power" and the success of Cory Aquino in the Philippines have given some in South Africa a model they wish to emulate. There are a number of critical differences, however, between the two situations. The first rests with the loyalty of the armed forces. Ken Owen, a South African journalist and frequent critic of the SADF, believes that, "the loyalty of the army is beyond question."[17] It is inconceivable that Defense Minister Magnus Malan would abandon the government and throw his weight (and the army's) behind a mass mobilization effort led by the ANC or UDF. A more likely scenario might be found with what occurred in Rhodesia. At the end of 13 years of bitter armed struggle, the

Rhodesian army was more than 70 percent black, yet remained totally loyal to the Salisbury command. It is difficult to imagine the SADF playing an active role in assisting or joining a mass mobilization.

The second problem with a successful national mobilization effort that would achieve revolutionary results is the lack of rudimentary economic stability that appears to be necessary for semi-industrialized societies to "mobilize." In the Philippines, for instance, it was the middle-class and business community that could afford to mobilize. As Tom Lodge explained,

> For many blacks who are economically struggling in the urban townships, to lash out at the powerful state is a luxury that simply doesn't exist. The "average" black man is too busy earning a living, providing for his family.[18]

Finally, much of South African society will be hesitant to participate in a mass insurrection because it could well open the door to the destruction that, for many, is too ghastly to contemplate. The national psyche is fully aware of the "worst case scenario," and a mobilization effort could lead not to a relatively short and peaceful revolution but, rather, to an increase in cyclical violence that could erupt into the destruction of their society.

The final criterion for a just revolution attempts to look at the "facts on the ground," the likelihood of the revolutionary movement succeeding. It calls for a "reasonable" chance of success, for there have never been guaranteed revolutionary victories (or defeats). In fact, many revolutionary efforts have looked rather feeble and produced highly successful results.

The South African scenario has some unique factors which must be considered in assessing the chances for an armed revolution victory. The current South African government is locally based among 4.5 million whites. It is not a distant colonial or metropolitan power. The SADF is the largest, most sophisticated armed force on the continent of Africa. Quantitatively and qualitatively the South African military overwhelms any force the ANC can muster. From a regional perspective the ANC cannot expect any long-term significant assistance from the front-line states that would allow it to establish bases or territorial "safe zones" within South Africa. The SADF is quite prepared to extend an armed conflict into neighboring sovereign states. Without direct outside supply routes, military logistics for the armed revolution become extremely difficult at best. It is not within the foreseeable future that a guerrilla (or freedom fighting) army could live off the countryside, fed by a conduit of arms from abroad.

An unquestionably loyal army; an apparent disinterest and economic inability in the black community; a national psyche that understands the horrors of a scorched earth policy: all contribute to the unlikelihood of a successful internal mass insurrection. The "people power" phenomenon remains outside the realm of near-term possibilities.

This fifth and last criterion forces one to think about the unthinkable. In the South African context an armed revolution could very well escalate and transform itself into the genocide of a race war—blacks and whites killing indiscriminately on the basis of skin color alone. The unthinkable is thought of, probably every day, by many who live in a world that has the potential for ghastly violence. As the late Alan Paton once said, "I think if there were such a battle, the black people would lose; it would be too horrible a thing to contemplate."[19] Because the just-revolution tradition will not tolerate the squandering of human life, it forces us to consider realistically the chances of a revolution's success. In the South African context, there is not a reasonable chance of an armed revolution being victorious, and if it did succeed, the victors would reign over ashes.

Seven

Just Revolution
The Criteria Are Not Fulfilled

As a tradition of the church, the just-war criteria provide Christians with an extremely useful body of moral wisdom and practical experience, helping us to discern when it is justifiable to resort to revolutionary violence. Relating this wisdom to the exigencies of our time is what makes the tradition a living and relevant theory.

The just-war tradition is a minimalist tradition. When extended to revolutionary situations, the five "ad bellum" criteria do not simply make up a laundry list of pluses and minuses for when a revolution is justifiable and when it is not. The tradition's goals and strategies all center around *tranquillitas ordinis,* Augustine's notion of the tranquillity of order. The theory is a set of constraints and hurdles, all of which must be addressed adequately if minimal conditions are to be met for initiating a revolution.

Implicit in the tradition is the understanding that all of the criteria must be fulfilled. This is not to suggest that the just-revolution theory is a sort of quadratic equation. Like any theory dealing with human society, it is an effort at approximation. There are times, as most just-war theorists have suggested, that circumstances prevent all of the criteria from being explicitly met, yet the revolution obviously can be considered "just." The Anglican theologian John Macquarrie suggests, "Sometimes in this distorted world there will be found conditions that to leave them unchecked would be an even greater evil than to employ the violence of war for their removal."[1] The tradition does, however, lay out five "ad bellum" criteria for us to apply present-day scenarios, measure and assess them, and arrive at conclusions. The first two criteria—

revolution due to real injury and revolution by a legitimate authority—are closely intertwined. In the South African context the Pretorian government does indeed cause real injury to the very people it claims to represent. South Africa today is only a democracy for 29 percent of the population, and such a "quasi-democracy" cannot claim full legitimate authority. This illegitimacy of the current South African government does not, however, result in the African National Congress automatically emerging as the legitimate authority; it clearly is not. The ANC, one of two violent revolutionary movements within South Africa, represents a sector of South Africa's black population, but it is not the only authority vying for power and certainly not the sole "legitimate" one.

Because of Pretoria's moral illegitimacy and the lack of any sole legitimate revolutionary elite, there is, in fact, a moral vacuum. This is not to be confused with a power vacuum—the South African government clearly dominates in that realm. This moral stalemate will not be resolved over night. It is up to South Africa's reconcilers to resist the current polarizing trends and fill that moral vacuum with a legitimate government.

The third criterion examines the revolutionary elite's goals and visions for the future. From the viewpoint of the post-Enlightment tradition of liberal democracy along with the traditional Christian values of justice, freedom and peace, the ANC's past goals are neither admirable nor commendable. Its visions have been dominated by Marxist and neo-Marxist rhetoric involving nationalization and expropriation of South Africa's wealth. In the past, the ANC's commitment to democracy was often understood within the Marxist framework that the success of the revolution justified everything. The ANC's violent "people's war" would most likely manifest itself at the expense of justice, liberty and peace for all South Africans. In the recent past, however, the armed revolution as the primary guiding principle has been challenged by those in the leadership who truly seek a multiparty democracy via negotiations. The ANC's visions for the future have changed, just as the organization itself has changed since 1912. The old violent visions of the 70s and 80 cannot be endorsed, but there is hope in the Congress's new vision of a multiparty democracy for a post-apartheid South Africa.

The fourth criterion, revolution as a last resort, is not adequately filled. All peaceful channels have not been exhausted. The greatest political victories achieved by the black community have come via nonviolent, usually economic, strategies and tactics. (The ANC's recent focus and reassessment of negotiations affirms this course.)

The vehicle of negotiations remains as an opportunity whose time seems to have come, or at least appears closer than ever. The KwaZulu-Natal Indaba and provincial and local negotiations like it remain as viable alternatives to an armed revolution. The radical metamorphosis within Afrikanerdom's elite indicate that there is a very real possibility that radical political change is in process within South Africa. Perhaps now more than ever, the possibility of a peaceful transition to a just and democratic society is evident. There remain a variety of potentially fruitful avenues to effect changes. The resort to violence is not justified given the nonviolent options which are now available and the success of nonviolent tactics now being employed.

The fifth and final hurdle that must be cleared asks a very practical question: Does the revolution have a reasonable chance of success? In the South African context, the answer is no. Although there are never guarantees that an armed revolution or a mass mobilization will succeed, a movement's chance of being victorious must be measured in realistic terms. The South African Defense Forces are the largest, most sophisticated armed forces on the continent; the neighboring front-line states could only offer limited logistical support for the ANC's "Spear of the Nation" army; and it is not within the foreseeable future that a guerrilla army could live off the countryside, even if it was partially supported by a stream of arms from abroad. If some mysterious string of events led to an ANC victory, the victorious would rule over a wasteland, for the conflict would produce a virtual desert.

Thus, although the criterion of "real injury" is met and the requirement for "legitimate authority" may be partially fulfilled, and the questions of the ANC's goals and visions are in flux, the other two criteria are not satisfied. As of the late 1980s, the violent revolutionary movement, led by the ANC, cannot be justified.

It is important to note that some Christians who support the ANC approach the use of violence not from the just-war tradition, but rather they seem to use concepts out of the medieval "crusade" tradition. The "holy war" or holy cause is the eradication of white power, symbolized by apartheid. A belief in "divine guidance" and aid is insinuated in the radical Left's critiques and evaluations.[2] "Godly crusaders and ungodly enemies" is manifested in the revolution's characterization of the South African government as completely and totally wicked. The "unsparing prosecution" is exemplified by the ANC's commitment to extremely violent tactics, either carried out directly or sanctioned for others to pursue. However, it is interesting to note that the increasingly "religious" ANC recently named an official chaplain, and Oliver Tambo often speaks in terms of the ANC as abiding by "Christian traditions."

If the revolution is not "just," yet the present ruling regime is not morally legitimate, what are the other options? Who and what will fill the vacuum?

The second part of this study will examine the choices that face South Africa—the choices between the system of apartheid and the violent revolutionary option of overthrowing it. There is indeed a third option between the status quo and armed revolution. That third way is a "middle ground," one that promotes democracy and economic freedom without resorting to armed revolution or settling for a tortoise-like pace toward reform.

Part II

The Democratic Middle Ground

What Are Its Prospects and How Can We Help?

Eight

Introduction to the Democratic Middle Ground

In the war of survival throughout history, all species have adopted one of two methods according to circumstances. One has been the beastly one of cruelty, murder and conquest. The other has been creative adjustment to new situations.

—Bishop A. H. Zulu

The vast majority of South Africans, black and white, want neither the apartheid of those who presently rule South Africa, nor the violence of those who rule the ANC. It is via this majority that the "middle ground," the third option, will find the support needed for a "creative adjustment" of which Bishop Zulu speaks and which is so desperately needed in South Africa. Shortly before his death novelist Alan Paton insisted that

> there is still a very great, almost anonymous center of people who just want peace and want to send their children to school, want to dress them properly, live a life of relative peace, and that's very strong among black people, white, Indian, and coloured people.[1]

Holding that center together, however, will not prove to be easy. The pessimism of the Irish poet Yeats is the challenge to be overcome.

> Things fall apart; the center will not hold:
> The best lack all conviction, while the worst
> are filled with passionate intensity.

There are no automatic solutions to the problems that lie ahead. What is required is patience, perseverance and, perhaps above all, faith and hope. Although the radicalization of the black and white communities has really only been effective on a large scale since 1984, the polarization within South Africa appears to be widening. The center seems to be dwindling. If the middle-ground agenda is to succeed, now is the time; 10 or 15 years from now could well prove to be too late. Ernie Wentzel, a white South African attorney who was active in the old Liberal Party, echoed Yeats' warning." The center ground tends to be eroded by extremists who have simplistic views about the situation, talk in rhetoric (and very loudly), and tend to take the center of the stage."[2]

The political dynamics of South Africa will not stand still long enough for a slow reform process to evolve. The moderates in South Africa do not have decades to achieve their goals and they know that. Chris Saunders, President of Tongaat Sugar, predicted,

> Before the year 2000, South Africa will be governed by a (racially) mixed government, Marxist, and oppressive; or by one that is mixed, capitalist and relatively free. The common denominator is that it is going to be mixed.[3]

There are a number of factors within the political, economic and social spheres that are influencing and shaping what post-apartheid South Africa is going to look like. We have assessed the ANC's and the South African government's visions, strategies and tactics; it is time to examine the activities and goals of the middle ground—the reformers, the liberals, the democrats.

Chapter 9 will discuss a major enemy of the authentic liberals: the romantic revolutionaries. Often coming from within the ranks of liberalism, these students of radical chic are betraying the goals and visions of a liberal, democratic South Africa. They have succumbed to the language of violent revolution and turn a blind eye to gross injustices and signs of totalitarianism in the revolutionary movement. The romantic revolutionaries pose a serious threat for the liberals in that they not only confuse the middle ground, but they encourage undemocratic and often vicious behavior that increases South African society's polarization.

From a more positive perspective, the 10th chapter will explore other factors that assist the democrats as they strive for radical change:

1. Economic growth and the business community's role in attacking apartheid remains one of the most effective methods of precipitating genuine reform. Annual earnings have shifted dramatically, resulting in black workers gaining economic power, which readily converts to political leverage.

2. Negotiations are at the cornerstone of the liberals' platform. Economic development, reconciliation and democratic education culminate in effective, genuine negotiations. The most hopeful living example of negotiations is the Indaba—the provincial constitution and Bill of Rights drawn up by a multi-racial convention in KwaZulu and Natal. The Indaba (Zulu for "high council") is a vital step toward negotiated reform and one whose development should be carefully tracked.

3. The religious community's role in South Africa has repeatedly been defined as critical. With 80 percent of the population calling itself "Christian," it is apparent that the churches have an important and powerful influence on South African society. The task of reconciliation finds its nourishment within prominent sections of the South African church world. Can the churches strengthen the notion of reconciliation before radicalization undercuts their efforts? Can the process of reconciliation find broad support within the political realm?

4. Another dilemma that faces the genuine liberals within South Africa is the understanding of democracy. When the majority of a nation's people have been denied the right to vote, promoting democratic ideals becomes a massive education problem. A multi-party democracy is an elusive concept to describe when it is impossible to point to any viable local examples.

The final chapters will suggest ways in which Americans can assist in bolstering the South African liberal agenda. Our influence, through both the government and the private sector, is clearly limited. We must understand and address the complexities of assisting a multi-racial nation toward full democracy. Various U.S. government policies and legislation will be suggested, as will examples of how the private sector can reinforce and help promote the difficult tasks that lie before the reformers of South Africa.

In a highly politicized society such as South Africa, certain language frequently becomes the calling card of various organizations. In the recent past, labels such as "moderate" could earn one a necklace. "Liberal" has such a wide variety of connotations (from being a Marxist to being a reactionary) that it is almost safe again to use. For our purposes a "moderate" is one who finds apartheid evil and the current policies of the South African government unjust, yet holds in disdain any form of Marxist totalitarianism that threatens not only freedom but justice and peace as well. A moderate, in this sense, neither supports the revolutionary violence of the ANC nor acquiesces in the structures of apartheid.

The label "liberal" in South Africa today represents those men and women who aspire after multi-party democratic systems that allow for economic imagination and freedom. Totalitarianism, from either the Right or the Left, is held in disdain. If such a system were permitted to reemerge or replace the existing order, the liberals will have failed. The *Business Day* editor Ken Owen, rather cynically commented,

> It was my misfortune to be born in South Africa at a time when the future rulers were seduced by the totalitarian ideas of the Right. I seem destined to die in a South Africa whose future rulers have been seduced by the totalitarian ideas of the Left.[4]

If the middle ground can activate its majority support, if authentic liberal leaders will emerge, if processes such as the Indaba continue, if reconciliations can occur on all levels, if outside support (particularly from the United States) can be formulated in such a way as to bolster the moderates, then Ken Owen will not have to be buried in a South Africa that is governed by the totalitarian Left. South Africa has a third alternative, a democratic future where the people need fear neither the sjambok nor the necklace.

Nine

Romantic Revolutionaries
The Slide-Away Liberals

*When our police rampage, that "is to be expected." We
know how to handle it, by gathering allies and protesting.
But when our own colleagues condone a necklace murder
by mentioning it only apologetically, or in small print on
page 4 of the newspaper, or preface their horror by long
lectures about understanding why it happens, then our
whole image of the world goes awry.*

—Jill Wentzel

There is a certain aura about revolution; it seems to make
everything understandable. It is concrete and exciting. It connotes
death and birth, injustice yielding to justice, and the sweet taste of
revenge. Revolution is enticing, and it is little wonder that the
liberal South African community has yielded up some of its most
dedicated leaders to that attractive allurement.

The romantic revolutionaries are indeed "slide-away liberals,"
often fueled by high-octane guilt. They have slid away from the
goals, vision and principles for which they once so dedicatedly
worked.

The slide-away liberals have embraced the revolutionary
movement's goals and tactics for a variety of reasons. There are
some who, in their fight against apartheid, felt it was mandatory
to hold more radical positions simply because it was a sign of
solidarity, a oneness with those also fighting the injustice of
apartheid. As a leader in the Black Sash tried to rationalize,

In order to maintain access to many of the black leaders, you simply cannot condemn violence in general. I might condemn a specific act, like a necklacing, but to make a general statement is to shut the door, cut off your access.[1]

Unfortunately, such slide-away liberals place a supreme importance on "maintaining access" to the revolutionary Left at the expense of justice and any notion of democratic ideals. Jill Wentzel, a white South African long involved in liberal politics and one who has recognized and is greatly concerned about the abandonment of genuine liberal principles, suggests,

It seems to me that some of the liberal people, who believe so profoundly in the rule of law, tend to lose sight of the relation between means and ends just at the very moment when it is most important that they do not do so.[2]

Opposing authoritarian violence and intimidation from the Right has, in the past, correctly been the focus of the liberal agenda. To alter radically the South African government's policies and to work for the abolition of apartheid and the creation of an authentic democracy was, and remains, the *raison d'etre* of the liberal community. But to do so by turning a blind eye to the terrifying tactics of the revolutionary movement is setting a course that may well lead to the end of apartheid, but at the cost of ushering in a potentially more unjust system. South Africans such as Jill Wentzel have recognized this phenomenon.

The government's responsibility for the present situation is obvious. At the same time we cannot be blind to the horrors of reactive violence which, however understandable, can only lead the country into the mire as it develops its own impetus, ideology and vested interest. When liberal human rights organizations become too timid to confront this type of violence, this is an ominous sign that society is doomed.[3]

A second type of slide-away liberal is depicted by the people who, because of their abhorrence of apartheid, largely wrap themselves in the rhetoric supplied to them by the revolutionary movement. This blind acceptance of rhetoric is not only naive, but it also encourages an unwillingness to remain faithful to liberal reason. (It may seem presumptuous for an outsider to label anyone who earnestly struggles for a better society as naive. Yet it is difficult to explain why the natural analysis that should occur seems to be passed over when it comes to assessing the overtly violent principles of certain "liberation movements.") As one liberal South African suggested,

> Some of the slide-away liberals have rehearsed the radical chic cliché so they know it by memory: 'How dare we, sitting in our comfortable white suburbs, criticize blacks who are driven to defensive violence by institutional violence?'[4]

Jill Wentzel wonders if these white liberals turned radical ever

> stop to find out whether the mass of ordinary black citizens who suffer most from the tactics of violent coercion would agree with them. They seem to talk instead to a black elite whose livelihood is assured (quite often from overseas).[5]

Ironically, the "black elite" is often substantially influenced by radical whites, thus removing themselves that much further from their constituents.

Part of the slide-away liberals' myopia manifests itself in non-recognition of the existing politics of coercion. Coercion has no color line, though it is far more harsh for the black community than for the white. In certain white circles there might be an expectation that you show certain forms of support for "liberation," such as giving money to the UDF or the End Conscription Campaign. But in the black townships, coercion means anything from forcing a worker to stay home during a work strike to the infamous "necklace." The knock on the door in the middle of the night must be answered. If the comrades demand your presence at an all-night rally, you go with them. Coercion is a reality that cannot be ignored.

The rhetoric of the neo-radicals in South Africa is attractive and sometimes difficult to criticize simply because they are committed to a worthy cause: the destruction of apartheid. Their utter commitment to that goal frequently causes them to ignore the very people—all South Africans—that they are attempting to assist. A liberal South African writes to a romantic revolutionary friend,

> You speak of peace, justice and democracy, I almost cannot bear to read these words any more; too many violent people have spoken them at too many meetings and funerals: they have come to sound like some terrible threat . . . those authors, philosophers, politicians who have done best for the human race, done best for peace, justice and democracy, have

hardly used these words, certainly not cheapened them by using them as slogans time and time again. Anyway, I don't want to work for peace, justice and democracy: I want to work for Mina to be able to decide whether she wants to boycott shops or whether she wants to take groceries home to her children, for Johannes Ndebele to be able to go to school because he happens to want to.[6]

The Consequences

Why is the romantic-revolutionary factor important in South Africa's formula to promote a middle ground? The consequences of the slide-away liberals' positions and actions discourage a truly democratic, post-apartheid South Africa. In the long-run, the radicalization of these liberals fosters ideologies and visions that may well pave the way for totalitarianism in South Africa. A South African journalist writes,

> The temper of the times is a compound of utopianism and violent obsession. Debate is dominated and the agenda set— by people who preach Marxist ideas with innocent fervor as though Budapest and Prague never happened and as though the self-correcting democracy of the United States is some-what a lesser institution than the militarism of the Soviet Union and Cuba.[7]

In the short-term, the romantic revolutionaries cause considerable damage to the efforts of liberalism and reconciliation by explicitly and implicitly categorizing the revolution as "right around the corner." Just how damaging this rhetoric is became evident with the black school boycotts and the call for "liberation before education." The rationale put forth by the radicalized liberals was that, since the revolution was only days or months away, the children could well afford to stay out of school. As a result thousands of children may have fallen irretrievably behind in their education.

Slide-away liberal rhetoric and tactics have also seriously hindered the process of negotiations. Often the neo-radicals refer to the Pretoria regime as "the evil system." They go on to suggest that one cannot negotiate with such evil—only confront it. Reverend Alan Boesak explained to a Black Sash Conference: "Non-cooperation with evil is as much a moral obligation as is cooperation with good."[8] Indeed there is much that can be judged evil in the structures and policies of the present government; however, this polarizing rhetoric does not aid the process of changing them. Pronouncing irrevocable damnation on the National Party does not facilitate later negotiations with it. On the contrary, it tends to rationalize the violent option.

W.P. Esterhuyse of Stellenbosh University defined the romantic revolutionaries of South Africa as "conveniently radical." That is, they have the convenience of holding romantic and frequently utopian view points (although with a bloody tinge) because they are secure in their white suburbs or in their foreign-funded vocations. He suggests that "the conveniently radical crowd acts as if they are attempting to buy a place in a Marxist heaven."[9]

Would these primarily white, upper-middle-class neo-radicals remain faithful to the revolutionary movement if it ever did arrive at their doorsteps? Or if the revolution did succeed would it allow these romantics to play a role? Would they be branded bourgeois intellectuals and activists and be ignored, or worse? The depth and degree of the commitment and influence of armchair revolutionaries is much in doubt. Their support or acquiescence to the revolutionary rhetoric, however, has been and will continue to be, a major roadblock for the liberal middle ground. How can those who recognize the threats of both the Left and the Right resist polarization and pursue liberal ideals? It will not be easy, but the liberals of South Africa must stand up and take it from all sides. In his crisp, somewhat cynical style, Ken Owen wrote,

> I am afraid liberals are suffering a collapse of nerve in the face of the pressure from the left, yet there was a time when South African liberals had the courage to fight on the retreat, to lose every battle, and yet hang on. It is time they recovered something of that courage to exploit new opportunities, the unintended consequences, which have been created by some of P.W. Botha's reforms. The prospects—let us be honest— are less bad than they were in the terrible days of granite apartheid under Verwoerd and Vorster.[10]

One of South Africa's most distinguished black journalists, Aggrey Klaaste, editor of the *Sowetan,* has written,

> It is time to have the guts to read political gangsters the riot act. We have been treating the violence sparked by political opportunism with kid gloves for just too long.[11]

South African liberals must to continue to condemn detentions, but they also need to go farther. They need to denounce the dangers on the radical Left just as they do those on the Right. Only then can they be faithful to their liberal ideals. Furthermore, the middle ground needs to develop a strategy, an explanation that sheds light on why today's jailers need to cease believing that prison is what protects them from being tomorrow's imprisoned. This strategy will need the assistance from the economic world, the religious community and from those parties who are willing to enter into negotiations.

Ten

Inside South Africa

Why the Democratic Middle Ground Has a Chance

Despite the polarization spawned by both the reactionary Right and the revolutionary Left inside South Africa today, there are developments that bode well for a democratic future. Both macroeconomic and microeconomic forces are playing a critical role in undermining the injustices of apartheid. The South African church world, some parts more effectively than others, is demonstrating its vision of the future by providing forums for reconciliation. In the political field negotiations have moved from a hope to a reality in the form of second-tier discussions such as the Indaba. The economic, religious and political components of South African society all offer opportunities for a non-revolutionary but radical departure from the apartheid system and an adoption of a new nation based on full democracy, tolerance and economic freedom. It is under these three pillars of society that the South African democratic middle ground can flourish.

THE ECONOMY

*Do you remember that lovely story in Jeremiah, chapter
32? When everything was going to rack and ruin around
him, Jeremiah did an odd thing. He goes and buys land as
a sign that it is going to be all right.*[1]

—Archbishop Desmond Tutu

Desmond Tutu is quite perceptive in retelling the Jeremiah
story, for it represents how a positive economic act can send
signals and precipitate actions throughout a society. To suggest that
economics alone will destroy apartheid and usher in a new nation
is to follow a dialectic that ultimately is insufficient. However, to
ignore or minimize the economy's role in building a post-apartheid
South Africa would be folly. What began cracking the Verwoerdian
wall of apartheid was not some guilt-provoked goodwill on the part
of the ruling Afrikaners; rather, it was economics. The rapid
economic growth of the 1960s and 1970s has become the catalyst
for political change since then.

Black Economic Empowerment

The tenet that apartheid will wither as the economy grows has
been coined the "Oppenheimer Thesis," after its architect, Harry
Oppenheimer of Anglo American, South Africa's largest corporation. Although revolutionaries and reactionaries alike have
rejected it, and many others have noted its incompleteness, the
thesis is essentially correct. The breakdown of apartheid has come
initially and primarily through the economic sector. Job reservation, the practice of preserving certain employment opportunities
for whites only, has been scrapped. Black trade unions have been
legalized and are growing rapidly. Real income for black workers
has increased significantly, allowing for increased purchasing
power and altering marketing shares in a wide range of goods and
services.

John Kane-Berman of the Institute on Race Relations
describes the economy as one of the principal avenues for attacking apartheid's "soft underbelly." When, in the early 1970s, the
white labor pool dried up because of rapid economic growth, the

private corporations simply ignored job reservation laws and began training black people for skilled jobs. The industrial color bar soon collapsed, which was followed by the official recognition of black trade unions. The economic realities also forced the granting of free hold home ownership rights and the scrapping of Influx Control (pass laws). This process began and continues primarily because the private sector ignores certain apartheid legislation. Certain economic axioms directly clash and are incompatible with apartheid laws, and economics inevitably prevails. Apartheid becomes unenforceable in these various economic relationships, and then it is only a matter of time until the legislative reform catches up with the economic realities. John Kane-Berman suggests,

> Employers who were short of skilled white workers simply trained blacks for the jobs, with the result that the laws against it increasingly became a dead letter.[2]

A senior minister in the Pretoria government said privately that companies had made a major contribution to change "when they just pressed ahead despite our silly job reservation laws."[3]

This attitude of ignoring official apartheid law because of economic realities manifested itself in the recognition of black trade unions. The South African government forbade the private sector to negotiate with any black unions. A few employers recognized the authentic need for black unions within the highly industrialized sector of South Africa's economy and began preliminary talks with the unions. More corporations began negotiating with the "unofficial unions," and before long the government enacted legislation that recognized them. Paving the way for the abolition of the Pass Laws was the economic necessity of people living and working in areas that were supposedly "prohibited." The repeal of the Pass Laws was simply an acknowledgment of reality; hundreds of thousands of people were moving to urban areas. Even the public sector ignored the apartheid law when, in Cape Town, the state-owned South African Transport Services turned a blind eye to the Pass Laws and offered non-whites jobs illegally.[4] The Group Areas Act will most likely follow the same course, thanks to economic realities that encourage or necessitate integrated housing.

It has been suggested that apartheid is like a huge onion; each time one layer is peeled off it exposes another. Economic pressure and necessity began the peeling process. What is now needed, as the "core of the onion" begins to be exposed, is an orchestrated effort by the private sector to continue to promote specific economic programs and be ready to replace apartheid's failed practices with new nonracial ones. This opportunity rests at the doorstep of both South African corporations and foreign companies. (The role of the U.S. corporation will be further examined in chapter 12.)

The unraveling of apartheid via the economic sector could not have occurred (and will not occur) in a stagnant or declining economy. The white labor pool would never have dried up if the economy had not been growing. The corporations would not have breached the law and negotiated with black unions if there had not been a rise in production requirements. As Helen Suzman puts it: "A contracting economy does not bring out the best in people. An expanding economy would bring blacks into the economy and give them greater power and muscle."[5]

Economist Gavin Maasdorp of the University of Natal finds great promise in the growth potential of the South African domestic market.

> Unlike Australia, for instance, South Africa's internal markets have very real growth potential, and the most effective and quickest way of blacks climbing the earnings and occupational ladders is via general economic growth.[6]

Black involvement in the South African private sector has increased significantly within recent years. In 1970 black-owned companies represented only 1.5 percent of all registered firms in South Africa. By 1985 there were 50,000 black-owned companies, which equaled 10 percent of all registered firms. Since 1985 it has been estimated that black-owned companies have increased at the fastest rate in South African history.[7] The non-white share of total disposable income rose by 12.2 percent between 1980 to 1985, while the white share fell by 17.9 percent during the same period.[8] By 1986, according to the U.S. Secretary of State's Advisory Committee, blacks comprised more than 40 percent of the "professional work force."[9]

Former U.S. Assistant Secretary of State Alan Keyes has suggested that "South African blacks have achieved their greatest victories over the apartheid system in the modern economic sector of the South African economy."[10]

Within some sectors of the South African economy the scale of black economic empowerment has been astounding. For instance, 10 years ago there were no black-owned taxis. In 1984 the South African government permitted blacks to own and operate taxis and buses. There were more than 170,000 black-owned taxis (or "combies") in 1988, representing $1 billion in assets. The Southern Africa Black Taxi Association (SABTA) now represents more than 40,000 of South Africa's black taxi and mini-van owners. Since 1987 SABTA has been South Africa's largest non-government purchaser of gasoline.[11]

The "informal" economy has been growing exponentially in the past decade. With the deregulation of certain commercial and racial laws, most central business districts are now open to any shop owner or business person, regardless of race. There are no official figures on the informal sector, but the University of Cape Town's Brian Kantor estimates that the informal economy is as high as 40 percent over the official Gross Domestic Product (GDP). This sector of the economy is unrecorded, unlicensed and generally untaxed.[12] It has been estimated that three and a half to four million people in South Africa (primarily black) are engaged full or part time in the informal sector, creating an annual income of between R15 billion and R22 billion per year.[13]

Various trade organizations, such as the African Council of Hawkers and Informal Business (ACHB), builders associations, printers, tavern owners, taxi associations (SABTA) and undertakers have emerged to assist in organizational skills, marketing programs and—perhaps most importantly—as lobbying institutions that negotiate on various government levels over political and economic rights.

'Creative Erosion'

The South African Catholic Bishops Conference concluded a report on "economic pressure" by stating that "long after business has built the bridges, politicians will cross over."[14] But how can South African business accelerate the process of change? How does a strategy of "creative erosion," to borrow John Kane-Berman's term, actually work?

It works via private corporations expending their resources on programs that aggressively erode apartheid. When a black employee wants to live in a "white area," a company should be willing and anxious to assist him financially and in any other way necessary. British Petroleum of South Africa recently offered to spend R100 million to build a Cape Town suburb, on the condition that it be designated a multi-racial area, and finance the necessary schools, which would also be multi-racial. Although the government gave the plan a cool reception, programs and plans such as this demonstrate a serious financial commitment by the business community to press the government to dismantle its apartheid restrictions.

Housing remains a critical need within the black community, and recently the government recognized that the black housing shortage must be addressed, but it clearly needs the help of the private sector. British Petroleum's plan lays down the ground rules: the private sector will help, but racial restrictions must be dropped.

Another example of potential corporate involvement resulted from the lifting of the Influx Control laws. The scrapping of this apartheid legislation has unleashed a boom in the black housing market. Black-owned real estate and construction companies are now providing many working black families with new housing. To purchase a free-hold house, however, most black families (like most white families) must take out a mortgage. Thus far, however, the "building societies" or savings-and-loans have been willing to commit only a small percentage of their portfolios to black loans. To assist in the creative erosion of apartheid, South African banks and lending institutions are going to have to open their capital to more black lending. If they will not take that risk, then alternative financing, such as black-owned building societies funded by white financial institutions (both inside and outside of South Africa), should be encouraged. (There is one black-owned bank, the African Bank, and more such black-owned lending institutions must be developed.)

Within the housing sector, the Urban Foundation has been a dynamic and progressive force. Founded by business leaders, the Urban Foundation finances black housing projects throughout South Africa. In 1987 the Foundation budgeted R80 to R100 million for new black housing construction. Perhaps one of South

Africa's most effective lobbying groups, the Urban Foundation, was instrumental in pushing for black land ownership rights and the abolition of Influx Control laws. The Urban Foundation, and similar organizations within South Africa's private sector, do not acquiesce in apartheid or attempt to make apartheid "more comfortable." They are actively and effectively using their capital base to move all South Africans into greater participation in the market system. As economic involvement and power increases for the black population, so too will political leverage.

Within the agricultural sector, a number of "creative erosion" policies could be fostered by private agricultural firms and farmers. The Land Acts, apartheid legislation which restricts land ownership to "white" and "black" areas, must be undermined. Private foundations, funded by the corporate sector, could be established to enable black farmers or black companies to purchase land for agricultural purposes in the so-called "white areas." Low interest loans could be provided for the purchase of the land and followed up with agricultural extension training and assistance.

The South African Sugar Growers Association launched a very successful program in 1973 known as the Small Cane Growers Financial Aid Fund. It is not in the business of purchasing land for black sugar cane growers, but it does make available capital and assistance to those growers to develop fully the economic potential of their sugar cane lands. The fund operates on a revolving credit system, making loans available to black growers annually. By 1988 more than R30 million had been loaned by the Financial Aid Fund.

The democratic middle ground cannot look to the South African economy as the sole pack horse that will carry the burdens of the anti-apartheid campaign. It won't. But the economy will play a vital role in undermining apartheid. If the private sector, both formal and informal, increases its efforts of "creative erosion," it will not only bolster the black community's political leverage (and help destroy apartheid), but it will also build a foundation for South Africa's future economic freedoms. The democrats of South Africa must exploit apartheid's failures, and those failures have been very obvious in the economic realm. Those in the private sector who anxiously await a post-apartheid nation have recognized apartheid's vulnerability in the market place. To take advantage of this weakness, the market economy must grow, must include South

Africans of all races and must continue to undermine its natural enemy—apartheid—every step of the way.

NEGOTIATIONS

Perpetuity is implied, if not expressed, in the fundamental law of all national governments. It is safe to assert that no government proper ever had a provision in its organic law for its own termination.[15]

—Abraham Lincoln

Negotiating a major alteration in a nation's fundamental political power structure is an immense task. For the existing government (morally illegitimate or not), it is a matter of sailing between the Scylla of the reactive (and reactionary) defenders of apartheid structures and the Charybdis of distrust and suspicion felt by those who are attracted to revolutionary solutions. The call for negotiations must remain front and center for the liberals and democrats of South Africa. The existing power structure is built on social and political inequality, but the armed revolutionary strategy is equally unacceptable; negotiations must occur if South Africa is to engineer a third, fully democratic option. The U.S. Secretary of State's Advisory Committee appropriately concluded,

> Negotiations are not merely desirable, but unavoidable... Black and white South Africans must recognize that military means—whether aimed at revolution or repression—cannot alone resolve the present struggle, and that, in the end, neither black or white can live and prosper without the other.[16]

Negotiations are possible only at the point where both sides perceive advantage in them. If opposing parties each have significant elements within them that think they can "win" without making any concessions, then the time for negotiations remains in the future. Once the parties have concluded (or are approaching a conclusion) that victory, according to their parochial views, is unattainable, then negotiations can go forward in earnest. Dr.

Pierre du Toit, political science professor at the University of Stellenbosch, wrote,

> When two or more parties to a conflict decide that the conflict cannot be won unilaterally on respective terms, and seek to terminate it by means of a settlement because it would be mutually beneficial to do so, they commit themselves to bargaining.[17]

It is misleading and destructive to presume that there is only one general, all-encompassing negotiating session that can take place in South Africa. Ultimately there will indeed have to be a national, all-parties constitutional convention of some type. Until all parties see profit in such an endeavor, however, many other smaller, but significant negotiating forums must be opened. Contacts, dialogues and discussions on all levels between a wide spectrum of individuals and groups all build up the foundations for a negotiating process. These various preliminary negotiations take the form of everything from white businessmen and academics meeting with the ANC to a more substantial negotiating process such as the Indaba. These diverse forums will be examined shortly.

One caveat concerning negotiations: It is frequently assumed that no authentic reform can take place if it is not a by-product of negotiations. This assumption is false and can be damaging to the reform process. The U.S. Secretary of State's Advisory Committee on South Africa over-extends the scope of negotiations when it writes, "To be seen as legitimate, reforms must come as a part of a process of negotiations."[18] Reforms can (and have) resulted from unilateral decisions where no negotiations took place. Such reforms have often been the product of various pressures (including economic) and are manifestations of newly-discovered economic or political leverage. To assume that legitimate reform can be produced only by a negotiating process is inaccurate and overly confining.

The End Product

"What should the middle-ground liberals of South Africa strive for in the negotiating process? What might the negotiated "solution" for South Africa look like? Currently in view are a vast array of constitutional blueprints for a post-apartheid nation. Individual South Africans have been quite creative in devising schemes for racial power-sharing. Many rely on some form of devolution of power or decentralization in one form or another. Devising such constitutional frameworks is a critical step in any nation-building process—and nation-building is, in fact, the course upon which South Africa must embark. Foreigners can offer past experiences that might be instructive as South Africans negotiate a new constitutional dispensation. (More detailed proposals and actions on the part of the U.S. government and private sector will be addressed in chapter 11.) The democratic middle ground in South Africa must pursue these essential principles:

- the elimination of apartheid
- universal suffrage
- a federal system with checks and balances
- guaranteed individual rights and liberties, both economic and political.

The exact components of a negotiated constitution will be just that—negotiated. Nobody knows what the exact end-product will be. The negotiating process often takes twists and turns that could never be predicted. The give and take of bargaining produces compromises that are never any party's "first choice." If South Africans can be loyal to basic democratic principles which guarantee individual liberties and have an effective method of checking governmental power, then the exact political form, be it a Westminster model or something closer to a French or American system, is not of critical importance. This is not to suggest that detail is unimportant. It is, and, more often than not, it is where the devil resides. Democrats will have to be diligent in the constitution-writing process, and make sure that democratic principles and institutions are guaranteed.

Levels of Negotiation

According to a 1986 South African public opinion poll, 74 percent of the blacks interviewed favored "negotiations" over any other process. [19] With such a large majority of blacks (and an equal percentage of whites) wanting negotiations, why are they not taking place? In fact, they are. Negotiations, discussions, even drafting of second-tier consensus constitutions is occurring in South Africa today. The Pretorian government clearly has not been forthright, creative or devoted to the negotiating process. But the discussion and bargaining process has been in the making, albeit in a rather unsystematic manner. The goal and aspiration of the liberals of South Africa must be to facilitate a systematic negotiating process that results in democratic reform on a national level. The most obvious and successful of the recent negotiations has been the Kwazulu-Natal Indaba. This demonstration of cooperation and consensus building demands a close assessment.

Indaba

In March 1986 the Natal Provincial Council and the KwaZulu government jointly convened the KwaZulu-Natal Indaba. On April 3, 1986 delegates from 38 organizations representing a wide spectrum of opinions, ethnic groups and economic interests, took their seats in the auditorium of the Durban City Hall. Never before had South Africans of all colors and persuasions sat down to attempt such a negotiating experiment. The goal: to reach a consensus (or a near-consensus) on the formulation of a single legislative body to govern the combined territories of KwaZulu and Natal.

The process had begun with the extension of invitations to 47 organizations including political parties; cultural agencies; commercial, industrial and agricultural associations; and municipal governments. Of those invited 35 accepted full representation, and three opted for observer status. (The National Party was present during the Indaba as an observer.) Refusals came from both reactionary and radical groups. On the Right, groups refused to enter into a debate simply because it crossed the color line. The rejections on the Left, including the United Democratic Front (UDF), were initially puzzling. But Desmond Clarence, former Principal of the University of Natal and Chairman of the Indaba, explained why some on the Left refused to participate.

> It soon became clear that should the Indaba meet with any success, it would be detrimental to the extreme left-wing desire for a total hand over of power in a unitary state. Clearly, the philosophies of the Indaba and the radical Left were diametrically opposed. The Indaba aimed to bring about peaceful change through negotiation while the radicals wanted the complete disruption of every facet of life in South Africa as a means to their end.[20]

The Indaba began the negotiating process with an agreed-upon six-point outline:
- the need for a single political structure in the region;
- that the region should remain an integral part of the Republic of South Africa;
- the right of full and effective political participation for all the people of the region;
- the need to abolish legislation based on racial discrimination and accept the democratic principles of freedom, equality, justice, the Rule of Law and access to the law;
- the need for a society founded upon a free economic system and the provision of equal opportunities for all people, while providing protection for the rights of individuals and groups;
- the principle that legislative and administrative power should be devolved as much as possible.

The first proposals that emerged from the dialogue centered on drafting a bill of rights. What emerged after five drafts is an outline of a democratic, post-apartheid society. Individual guarantees include equality before the law; personal privacy; property ownership and occupancy; educational and linguistic rights. Other freedoms supported by the Indaba bill of rights are freedom of movement, of conscience and religion, of opinion and expression, of association and of work and contract. All rights and freedoms are to be legally guaranteed and enforceable through the Supreme Court.

Once the bill of rights was agreed upon (and published), the central task was to devise and evaluate different constitutional models. The final proposal was for a two-chamber legislature with a governor, a prime minister, a provincial executive, standing committees, cultural councils, traditional authorities and an economic advisory council.

- The first chamber would consist of 100 members elected by voters on the basis of universal adult suffrage. There would be no voting restrictions based on race or gender; it would be one man, one vote.
- The second chamber would consist of 50 seats made up of five groups each with 10 members. The five designated groups would be of the following backgrounds: Afrikaans, English, African, Asian and South African. Voters would be asked voluntarily to associate themselves with the group of their particular

background. Should a voter not fit into one of the first four groups, or if he or she did not wish to be classified in any way at all, the voter could then declare himself a member of the South African group. This "classification" is not strictly along racial lines; the English-background group, for example, could conceivably include English-speaking whites, coloureds and Asians.

• The provincial executive would consist of the prime minister, who would be the leader of the majority party in the first chamber, and 10 or more other ministers. Half of the ministers will be appointed by the prime minister from his own party and the other half elected by an electoral college consisting of the elected members of all the other parties in both chambers.

• A standing committee consisting of 15 members, would be established for each executive portfolio. The standing committee would be made up of members from both chambers.

Legislation would be initiated by the executive and sent to the appropriate standing committee. If approved, it would be placed before the first chamber; if passed, it would then move to the second chamber. All legislation would have to be passed by both chambers with a simple majority in each. As Peter Mansfield, Director of Communications for the Indaba, said, "We consistently heard delegations say, 'It's not our first choice, but we can live with it.'"[21] As Mr. Chris Saunders, a leading business executive in Natal, stated,

> What the bill of rights and proposed constitution means is that after eight months of negotiations, the Indaba reached a consensus that we are all South Africans, that we must all share a common society, and that individual rights come before group rights.[22]

The final draft proposal, as outlined above, was supported by 82 percent of the delegates; nine percent abstained, and nine percent voted against it. The Indaba is now awaiting Pretoria's approval for holding a referendum election (and assistance with voters rolls), open to all men and women over 18 years of age in KwaZulu and Natal. (A second, considerably less attractive alternative is to conduct a highly sophisticated public opinion poll throughout the region.)

The Indaba participants sense they have achieved something historic, yet they are anxious over the central government's position. Peter Mansfield explained,

We are trying to convince them (Pretoria) that if we're
going to ever find a plan that will solve the problems of Natal
or the rest of South Africa, it has to be a plan that has the
support of all the races. And this is the only plan, so far, that
is acceptable to all races."[23]

Pretoria has sent out conflicting signals, including a rather
premature dismissal by the chairman of the Natal National Party,
Stoffel Botha. Yet there still appears to be an underlying interest
in the Indaba among National Party leaders. One cabinet minister
called the Indaba "bloody exciting" and suggested it might become
the foundation for future negotiations. The new National Party
head, F.W. de Klerk, has apparently made favorable comments
concerning Pretoria's approach to it.[24]

The Indaba has suggested a potential constitution and bill of
rights for a province. It is a second-tier negotiation that proposes
solutions on the local and provincial level. KwaZulu and Natal
seem to be at the threshold of entering the post-apartheid era. What
increases the complexity of the solution, however, is that the
Indaba proposes local and provincial answers to national
problems. John Kane-Berman, of the Institute on Race Relations,
views it as such:

Local and provincial solutions do not pretend to be, nor
are they, substitutes for a national political solution, which
requires a national constitutional conference in which the full
range of South African political opinion would have to be able
to participate freely. Such a conference must be the key
objective, but the desegregation of government at local levels
will play an important part in bringing it about.[25]

The delegates and supporters of the Indaba fully recognize that
a new KwaZulu-Natal government and constitution would not cure
all of South Africa's political, social and economic ills. If the
Indaba were implemented, however, it would mean that roughly
25 percent of South Africa's population would be governed by a
multi-racial body and constitution.

Perhaps more importantly, as Peter Mansfield and others are
quick to note, the Indaba is creating "building blocks" for negotiations in other provinces and localities—perhaps, on a national
level as well. Oscar Dhlomo, one of the co-conveners of the
Indaba, explained,

Nobody in the Indaba has illusions that it meets aspirations of blacks on a federal or central level. We see it as a stepping stone towards total black participation in the central government.[26]

The Indaba's importance rests with the understanding that it represents a negotiating process that can arrive at realistic and authentic democratic alternatives to apartheid. It demonstrates to all South Africans and the global community that the negotiating process can be successful, even within the increasingly polarized society of South Africa in the late 1980s. The Indaba offers a model for other local and provincial (and possibly national) governments. It could not simply be extrapolated for other various government structures, but the procedure could be borrowed and modified. There have been initial multi-racial meetings in both the Western Cape and the Transvaal to examine the Indaba procedure and assess its applicability to those other regions.[27]

Certainly part of the Indaba's attraction and success was due to its local or second-tier nature. Chris Saunders and others often speak of South Africa's "two pyramids of power—political and industrial." One is represented by Afrikaner Pretoria and the other by English Johannesburg. The suggested thesis is that neither of these pyramids is willing to readily abandon its power or wealth. The answers for a post-apartheid democracy rest on the provincial and local levels. (Leon Louw and Frances Kendall's *South Africa: The Solution* also relies on a highly decentralized process, similar to the Swiss canton system.)[28] The fact that the Indaba is a local, not national, phenomenon makes it that much more likely to succeed.

In March 1987, a poll in KwaZulu and Natal was taken, measuring the level of the Indaba's support. Out of 3,500 questioned (all races) 75 percent supported it, 10 percent disapproved and 15 percent were undecided. (A racial breakdown showed approval among blacks by 13 to one; among whites by four to one; and Indians and coloureds by three to one.)[29] The Indaba faces some difficult hurdles ahead as the far Right and far Left continue to reject it. The National Party's attitude is critical in that it holds the key to allowing a regional referendum. The democratic middle ground must rally to the side of the Indaba proposals and encourage the ideals and principles that have arisen from the negotiations. The Indaba has started down the road to a democratic, non-racial South Africa, and the proposals brought forth by it must be nurtured and spread to other second-tier government structures. Eventually it must embrace a national dimension.

Other Discussions

Partially spurred on by the hope of the Indaba, other negotiations have been occurring within South Africa. Sheena Duncan, former President of the Black Sash, has exclaimed, "You would be astonished at the tremendous amount of negotiating going on."[30] Some of these discussions involve government officials. In May and June of 1986 high level meetings reportedly took place between the KwaZulu cabinet and P.W. Botha's cabinet. Shortly after the May 1987 elections Stoffel Van der Merwe was named Deputy Minister of Constitutional Development (cabinet rank), with an explicit mandate to investigate the negotiating process. Van der Merwe has expressed a willingness to meet with a wide variety of black leaders. In June 1987 he remarked,

> Not all of these people ('radicals') are ideologically committed to violence. People who use violence as a strategy are not necessarily excluded, because I think they can be persuaded.

He hinted that ANC leaders should be included.[31] Van der Merwe also declared that he was prepared to talk with imprisoned black activists to give new impetus to a possible negotiation process. He commented, "The mere fact people are in detention or have been in detention is not an absolute prohibition against talking to them."[32]

The Pretoria government's apparent willingness to "talk about talking" is possibly a good omen. Its devotion to legitimate negotiations, however, remains rather thin. The South African liberal community can and will continue to encourage, demand and cause the South African government to pursue honest attempts at significant political negotiations. Outside of Pretoria's involvement, there have been numerous attempts at initiating discussions on a variety of issues with a range of groups. By 1986 South African business, academic and church leaders had worn a wide path to Lusaka where they regularly consulted with ANC leaders. In July 1987, 65 South African businessmen, professors, farmers and politicians held talks with ANC leaders in Dakar, Senegal.

These and other efforts are laying the groundwork for future discussions. The Institute on Race Relations, for instance, has developed an extensive project that attempts to identify critical issues common to all interest groups across the political landscape. Once the issues have been clearly stated, the parties that are willing to enter the discussions must be identified. Although George Kennan's caveat—that the likelihood of any negotiations reaching agreement diminishes by the square of the number of parties taking part—has practical merit, all willing and interested parties must be considered.

A number of recent key negotiations on the municipal level have been particularly hopeful. In early 1989 preliminary negotiations began over the two-year rent boycott in Soweto. Opposition activists met with black municipal councilors who are charged with running Soweto. A general agreement was reached between the Rev. Frank Chikane, general secretary of the South African Council of Churches, and black Soweto officials that the $70 million in rent owed to the township would be forgiven. These discussions led to other meetings, including a series of negotiations in which Chikane participated, concerning the extension of electrical service throughout Soweto.[33]

These municipal level meetings between opposition activists and township and regional authorities appear to be rapidly increasing as a new and more pragmatic approach seems to be replacing the radical rhetoric of 1985 and 1986. A Johannesburg political scientist described this approach,

> This isn't a confrontation strategy designed to bring down the government. It's a negotiation strategy that will make gains through collective bargaining. And it will reinforce the idea that further negotiations could lead to even greater gains.[34]

The democratic middle ground in South Africa must continue to work for authentic discussions on all levels. As one black leader pleaded, "There is sunshine now—someday it will be sundown. Let us please work together in the sunlight, rather than in the darkness."[35]

Perhaps the sunlight will last longer than many expect; perhaps not. But the key to the birth of a new South Africa rests with realistic negotiations with parties that are committed to the give and take of bargaining. Perhaps the Pretorian regime, as well as the pretenders in Lusaka, have taken to heart only the first half of John F. Kennedy's statement on negotiation: "Let us never negotiate out of fear . . . but let us never fear to negotiate." The time for serious negotiations on fundamental power shifts on the federal level might soon be at hand. Although some parties still envision their own peculiar brand of victory as quite plausible, there seems to be a new willingness to seek out he other side's position. The "talks about talks" stage seems to be near.

At the heart of the negotiating process are individuals—men and women, often for the first time attempting to hammer out logically and peacefully an accord with others whom they have previously feared. Fear is what so often prevents negotiations. Fear is what reconciliation destroys, and fortunately for South Africa there is a committed group of reconcilers devoted to dispelling the darkness of fear.

RECONCILIATION:
THE ROLE OF THE CHURCHES

The whites hold the key to the black man's prison of anger, and blacks hold the key to the white man's prison of fear. Neither can get out without the other.[36]

—Michael Cassidy

Theologically the term reconciliation refers to a specific change of attitude from hostility to amity. This change can take place between an individual and God or between individuals. The concept is essentially a relational one that involves conversion and forgiveness. In the early church, reconciliation between the individual and the church occurred after a grave post-baptismal sin; it was only granted once in the individual's lifetime, and it held a place of unique importance within the life of the church.[37]

These theological and historical understandings of reconciliation can add depth to the modern term that is used (and abused) in today's political, economic and social circles. In the South African context, reconciliation is taking place between individuals, groups and communities. Reconciliation efforts that encourage a change of attitude from hostility to amity, from anger to understanding and from fear to hope, are occurring daily. Polarization, fueled by the revolutionary movement's armed struggle—as well as the government's reactive oppression—continues to spin in the opposite direction. Resisting the tide toward increased radicalization (on the Left and the Right) is not a simple task for the middle ground. Yet relations between individual South Africans exist and are developing which reflect concern and forgiveness. Reconciliation is occurring.

At the center of this effort are many South African churches. The U.S. Secretary of State's Advisory Committee on South Africa suggested,

> One of the most important potential forces for reconciliation across racial lines in a post-apartheid South Africa is religion. Nowhere else, not even in Poland, is religion such a pervasively important factor in the politics of a nation.[38]

It has been estimated that well over 75 percent of the South African Population belong to Christian denominations.[39] Religion remains a pillar of South African society. It has the potential to be the motivating force behind a moderating voice preaching forgiveness and transformation rather than armed rebellion.

Unfortunately, some church leaders have abandoned the reconciliation process and instead turned to the alternatives offered by the revolutionary movement. The stereotypes of the Dutch Reformed Church (NGK) as the "inventors and protectors of the theology of apartheid," the English-speaking denominations as "passive" or acquiescing in apartheid, and the radical churchmen behind the Kairos Document as "prophetic liberators" are incomplete and misleading. There are many churchmen and women who do not fit these stereotypes and who are promoting reconciliation without embracing either the existing regime or the violent revolutionary option. (See chapter five, concerning the Dutch Reformed Church.) To be sure, there are supporters and defenders of both the Pretorian government and the radical Left within the church world; their efforts will be examined shortly.

Reconciliation: The Theory

Klaus Nurnberger, Professor of Theological Ethics at the

University of South Africa, defines reconciliation as a process that moves South African society towards "horizontal" structure. That is, South Africa must move away from its "feudal-patriarchal" social nature, which is a vertical relationship, to a "liberal-competitive" social structure which is essentially horizontal. Nurnberger explains that in moving away from the feudal-patriarchal, or vertical structure, a tremendous amount of guilt will occur in the white population (see chapter 9). Numerous South African theologians (including Professor Johan Heyns of the NGK) suggest that the process of reconciling one person to another must be rooted in the individual's faith. The biblical understanding of reconciliation involves both transformation and forgiveness; a societal reconciliation will only be successful if it does not lose sight of these essential characteristics.

The process of conversion and forgiveness has already begun throughout South Africa. Reconciliation is under way, but it is a gradual process that initially works on an individual rather than group level. Dr. Nico Smith who initiated a group known as "Family Fellowship," stresses individual friendships.

> . . . the best thing to do now is to create personal relationships between the races in order to bridge the gap created by apartheid; we need to encourage people to discover one another.[40]

The best forum in which to begin the reconciliation process is in the churches themselves. The Dutch Reformed Church, in its October 1986 Synod, opened the way for reconciliation by denouncing apartheid and declaring that it cannot be biblically supported or encouraged. In March 1989 it described the apartheid ideology as sinful. (See chapter five.) In other Protestant and Catholic churches integrated services, weekend retreats focusing on reconciliation and training sessions in reconciliation techniques for church leaders are under way.[41] Professor W.P. Esterhuyse of Stellenbosch University believes that "the key to South Africa's future will be determined by what people do on the local level—the kinds of bridges built on that level, what takes place in the churches and in the pulpits."[42]

Church-based groups have started emerging with the sole intent of building bridges between individuals. The National Initiative for Reconciliation (NIR) was launched at a gathering in 1985 with 400 Christians from all racial groups and 48 different denominations. The NIR has brought blacks and whites together to worship, to discuss their differences and to meet human needs in both the townships and the suburbs. It has sponsored days of prayer and fasting and is currently involved in concentrated ministries of reconciliation for specific towns and cities. The NIR declares that its activities seek to "prepare people to live in a changed and totally nonracial land." As the Anglican Bishop of Durban, Michael Nuttall, proclaimed,

> The NIR and Michael Cassidy (its founder) have caused the rediscovery of God in all our Politics, and ultimately the solutions will come from Him. . . . Unless we go out of our way to build contacts, we will be locked in our separate corners. I think this is the key to the NIR and reconciliation in general.[43]

Among South Africans opting for radical change via reconciliation rather than through a Marxist-oriented revolution, there is a diverse understanding of exactly how individuals being reconciled with one another can produce a post-apartheid, democratic South Africa. Reconciliation clearly has a spiritual, individualistic element at its very core; it is a changing of attitudes. Perhaps reconciliation occurs most frequently during or after a negotiating process. The discussions and personal contacts made and developed during negotiating sessions can be the foundation for reconciliation. A South African journalist who closely followed the Indaba proceedings, for instance, commented, "The actual process of negotiations changed the people doing the negotiating."[44]

A bargaining process can often provide a forum for authentic reconciliation. History, however, favors a nation being more fully reconciled after a successful negotiating process has occurred. This is not to suggest that forgiveness and reconciliation must wait until negotiations are concluded. In fact, reconciliation will take place before, during and after a successful settlement. But to expect reconciliation to occur on a national level without the political process of a negotiated constitutional process is overly optimistic.

The vast majority of South African Christian leaders of all races are committed to reconciliation, as opposed to a violent revolution. But the South African church is not a unified body when it comes to defining goals and strategies for a post-apartheid nation. A closer examination needs to be made of the church world and how the churches assist or detract from the middle ground's efforts toward a democratic South Africa.

Varied Voices Among the Churches

In September 1985 a number of theologians published *The Kairos Document: A Theological Comment on the Political Crisis in South Africa.* The document identified three theologies within South Africa: "State Theology," "Church Theology" and "Prophetic Theology." The authors explain "State Theology" as the "theological justification of the status quo with its racism, capitalism and totalitarianism."[45] The Kairos theologians further suggest that appeals for law and order merely serve to "canonize the will of the powerful and reduce the poor to passivity."[46]

"Church Theology" is applied to those who seek reconciliation and a post-apartheid South Africa via nonviolent protest and negotiations. These Christians, according to the Kairos authors, are "sitting on the fence" and "playing into the hands of the oppressor."[47] The document identifies the main defect in "Church Theology" as "a lack of social analysis."[48]

Their solution, "Prophetic Theology," consists of their own "social analysis" which is firmly rooted in class conflict. They attempt to fit South Africa's racial conflict into the Marxist mold of a struggle between the capitalist elite and the exploited labor class. The document suggests that the "two classes" are "two conflicting projects and no compromise is possible."[49]

The "Prophetic Theology" postulates that South African whites, as a class with interests linked to the present system, will never "experience a conversion or a change of heart and abandon the policy of apartheid."[50]

Because of this assumed irreconcilable conflict which cannot be resolved through compromise, the Kairos writers articulate a "Challenge to Action."

> In opposition to tyranny and oppression Christians may be required to take solidarity action or join significant political movements working towards the overthrow of tyranny where clear Christian choices may not be possible or available. . . . The time has come for the churches to declare their alliance with the forces of liberation against the apartheid regime."[51]

They go on to insist that all church activities (including the sacraments) be done in "consultation, coordination, and cooperation" with "those political organizations that truly represent the grievances and demands of the people."[52] Exactly which "political organizations" the authors had in mind is only implicitly suggested. But it is clear that many of the Kairos theologians feel comfortable with the ANC's most violent activities and goals. The essential righteousness of "liberation movements" is never questioned in the document; the only criticism comes in commenting on certain "counter-productive" excesses. The Kairos Document is vague enough to provide room for some genuine democrats, but its approach, particularly the use of a "social analysis," which has inordinate similarities with Marxist analysis, is clearly in line with non-democratic, revolutionary movements.

The South African church world mirrors the full range of political ideologies that currently exist in South African society today. At a "Christian-Marxist dialogue," Michael Lapsley, an Anglican priest and member of the ANC, stated,"We Christians can but salute and be humbled by the dedication, commitment and self-sacrifice of our communist sisters and brothers."[53]

The other extreme is represented by the Dutch Reformed Church's new splinter groups known as the "Afrikaans Protestant Church." Willem Lubbe, spokesman for the newly-formed church, described his church as "a church of Christians among white Afrikaners."[54]

The middle ground must continue to encourage South African Christians to reject these two extremes and opt for a truly democratic third way. Unfortunately the ecclesiastical world is often as muddled as the secular one.

Church leaders should (and could) be articulating and broadcasting a liberal, democratic strategy and vision for the birth of a new society. Unfortunately some leading South African clerics have let their rhetoric expand into areas that one would hope they have later regretted. The Reverend Alan Boesak, president of the World Alliance of Reformed Churches, has come close to endorsing the armed revolutionary movement's agenda. In 1987 he told an American college audience,

> The inevitable conclusion is that, looking back now, we must say that in South Africa, every single non-violent effort over the past twenty-five years or so has ended in a massacre. We must come to the conclusion that in South Africa right

now, there is, through the actions of the South African government, no room left for nonviolent protest.[55]

Boesak concludes that there are only two options,

> You can either say because there is no room for nonviolent protest, we must now try to find other ways, preferably violent.... Or you must say that we have tried everything ... our people must accept our position. The first option, I still find extremely difficult to accept. The second option is quite impossible.[56]

The real tragedy in Boesak's conclusion is not so much in his opting for revolution (there are indeed "just revolutions"), but rather in losing hope for reconciliation and in legitimizing the violent revolutionary option. The Reverend Boesak and other Christian leaders seem to have reduced the Christians' options to one of two poles. They have abandoned the possibility of a middle ground.

To add to the South African church world's menagerie, there is what might be described as a "fourth option." Proponents of this option reject the revolutionary Left and the reactionary Right but refuse to get involved with the reconcilers of the middle ground. Their "solution" is to curse both houses and to look for an eschatological deliverance. This strain of theological separatism can frequently be found in numerous black and white independent churches. The number of apolitical Christians in South Africa is significant. Without attacking the independents' biblical understandings and commitments, the middle-ground democrats should encourage these Christians to participate actively in acts of reconciliation without necessarily becoming political activists. To characterize independent Christians actively working towards reconciliation as "fence sitters," as the Kairos Document does, however, is inaccurate and fails to recognize that expectations of a celestial solution might be as likely as any.

Can the South African church world assist the democratic middle ground in ending apartheid and replacing it with a system of liberties and freedoms based on democratic traditions? The answer is clearly yes. The church remains a pillar of South African society, and the vast majority of Christians are committed to replacing apartheid with a participatory democracy. South African society is a highly politicized one, and the influence of politics upon church leaders can be intense. There are Christians in the ANC and the AWB—that is why the process of reconciliation must begin within the churches themselves. Because of the supreme importance and magnitude of religion within South Africa, a reconciled church would go a long way in producing a reconciled nation.

The churches have already begun their work of reconciliation, and it has reaped some hopeful results which are optimistic harbingers. The National Initiative for Reconciliation is just one of many organizations devoted to the process. The change from hostility to amity, and the conversion and forgiveness which make up reconciliation can and will occur whenever and wherever there are willing parties.

Professor John Heyns tells a powerful story of what reconciliation has meant to him. As a young Afrikaner Heyns had little or no contact with multi-racial worship in the NGK. His church experience, like his schooling, was an all white one. As a graduate student in Holland, Heyns attended a Sunday communion service. Next to him was a young black man sharing in the body and blood of Christ.

The symbolism struck the young Heyns as both powerful and obvious. Here was a black person with whom he would "normally" never come in contact. But through Christ they were brothers who shared common goals, aspirations, fears and joys. He could come to know, understand and love this person through Christ. There is no doubt that Heyns' personal reconciliation that Sunday morning laid the foundation for his noble efforts in reforming the NGK.

Reconciliation can happen under the auspices of a wide range of forums: the church, politics, economics and sports, for example. It is within the political realm, specifically within the negotiating process, that reconciliation can make a particularly distinctive mark felt by an entire province or nation. Reconciliation during and after a negotiating process can make reform authentic and lasting.

The churches, despite the multitude of voices that frequently contradict one another, can be key agents in facilitating the negotiating process. Professor David Bosch of the University of South Africa sees the churches' role in contributing to the solution as unmistakable. "The church already has a network. It's a network that crosses all boundaries. Thus we can lead in negotiations; we can lead in reconciliation. . . ."[57] The chance for true freedom and democracy can be greatly enhanced by those Christians who persevere, despite polarizing circumstances, in the biblical ministry of reconciliation.

DEMOCRACY IN SOUTH AFRICA: WILL IT WORK?

Man's capacity for justice makes democracy possible; but man's inclination to injustice makes democracy necessary.[58]

—Reinhold Niebuhr

All liberal visions of a post-apartheid South Africa include democratic ideals and institutions. The alternative to a one-party, centrally-planned state with a command economy or the reactionary apartheid of the Pretorian regime is a solution which has democracy as its cornerstone. But by what means can a nation, where complete democracy has thus far been denied, develop the desired democratic institutions?

The Theory

For some, the very term "democracy" has waned in value, as virtually every political system and every nation on earth during the last half of the 20th century has claimed to be a democracy. After all, East Germany is formally known as the "German Democratic Republic," and the clearly non-democratic nation of South Yemen calls itself the "Democratic Republic of Yemen." Frequently these "admirers" and "professors" of democracy point to their constitutions, where indeed elections, parties and voting assemblies appear in print. Unfortunately the machinery of these governments is not consistent with democratic ideals or their own constitutions. These counterfeit democracies do not, however, discredit the ideals of democracy.

Democracy does not mean institutionalized mob rule; that is a form of fascism. Successful modern democracies are characterized by constitutional safeguards protecting minorities from the tyranny of the majority by regularly scheduled open elections and other measures which facilitate a peaceful turnover of power; by fundamental commitments to preserve the civil rights of all citizens; and by an institutional separation of powers via various forms of checks and balances.

Some have argued that democracy is not "exportable," and it is true that the transition to democracy in nations where there is little or no precedent for it has been anything but smooth.[59] Yet since the end of World War II, the world has witnessed examples of European, Asian, Latin American and African states embarking upon a democratic path. There is clearly reason for hope in South Africa.

The Practice

The difficulty of a nation moving away from authoritarianism (or totalitarianism) toward democracy is this: without freedoms, how can a people identify and peacefully pursue the establishment of a free government? The bulk of the South African population has not had an opportunity to resolve political conflict via the ballot box. Sheena Duncan worries that the

> notion of democracy, which involves power changing hands at regular intervals, is not understood by many. In other words, the idea of authentic elections doesn't seem to be fully grasped.[60]

As writers from Alexis de Tocqueville to Jacques Barzun have concluded, there are a "cluster of disparate elements" that usually hinge on the individuals' understandings of liberty, which make it possible for a nation to "grasp" democratic traditions. Many throughout the West, including Professor Klaus Nurnberger of the University of South Africa, have talked about the need for a "democratic spirit." He writes,

> Democracy presupposes a spirit—a spirit where people believe in freedom, in tolerance, in human rights, in equal dignity, in the public responsibility of all citizens, in authority located in the people who are ruled. All this cannot simply be taken for granted. Values have to be internalized through an educational program. And their application has to be learnt through practice."[61]

Democratic thinkers, like Nurnberger and others, frequently write and speak of "internalizing values" and "education in democratic traditions." These are the strategies that must be pursued if the third option is to prevail. For what de Tocqueville calls the "habits of the heart" to take root, there must be an education which nurtures democratic values and involves actual participation in the democratic process. There is an answer to the question, "How can people learn the ways of a free government?" But it does require a certain amount of time for that learning to occur. Historically, democratization is an incremental, often painfully slow process—a process which is frequently overtaken by other events and ideologies and which, unfortunately, often never reaches its conclusion. South African liberals face an extended project in attempting to foster democratic values and apply them in a practical manner. As one South African democrat explained, "Make no mistake, this is a long-term task, but the sooner we begin, the better for the country and all its people."[62] Many, of course, are convinced that the process has already been underway for sometime.

Some have asserted that neo-Marxism or a brand of "African socialism" is far closer than democracy to the tribal structure that has existed throughout the continent. However, the similarities between consensus decision-making under the traditional chiefs and the workings of a one-party Marxist state are few and far between. And the benevolence of the ethnic cultures in southern Africa bears no similarity with any existing Marxist systems. In economic terms, land use practices within tribal customs have a closer affinity with private ownership than with collectivization.

Alexis de Tocqueville and Klaus Nurnberger are correct—a spirit of democracy must capture the hearts and minds of all South Africans if the post-apartheid nation is to enjoy political equality and individual liberty. And there is no better educational forum for building an appreciation for democracy than involving the population in decision-making processes. Entering into local or provincial negotiations (such as the Indaba or the Soweto rent boycott discussions), being involved in market and business decisions and encouraging dialogue among Christians on current political or social issues—all are key elements in fostering understanding and appreciation for democracy.

Conclusion

It is the role of the true liberals in South Africa—those committed to democratic ideals, those who want to see a machinery of government in place which defends equality before the law and yet promotes personal freedoms—to educate society. This democratic educational process will be, and currently is being, conducted via the three primary spheres of South African culture that have been examined: economic, political (negotiations) and religious. The "soft underbelly of apartheid," as John Kane-Berman describes it, can be effectively attacked via the economic sphere. Political leverage is developed through economic power. Economic and societal changes currently underway are preparing the ground for meaningful negotiations. The Indaba, the most successful second-tier negotiation to date, can serve as a hope and a model for future endeavors. The religious community, given the depth and breadth of the churches' influence in South Africa, provides a forum for reconciliation. Although the churches represent the broad political spectrum within South Africa, the vast majority of church leaders and congregations are committed to reconciliation within the body of Christ, as well as within the whole of South African society.

The democratic middle ground has its work cut out for it. The "solutions" of the two extremes are simple and straightforward—reactionary authoritarianism based on racial injustice or armed revolution with a totalitarian state as the likely consequence. The middle ground must be equally bold and assertive: democracy must be given a chance to develop and thrive. The type of government, the kind of nation which will develop after apartheid, is in the hands of the South African people. Outside influence is limited and needs to be recognized as such. Yet there are areas where actions by foreign governments or overseas organizations can assist or hinder the middle ground's formidable task. The next chapters will examine how and why certain ideas, initiatives and programs of the U.S. government and the U.S. private sector can either serve as catalysts for democratic change in South Africa or hasten South Africa's plunge into the nightmare of violent confrontation.

Eleven

U.S. Foreign Policy Toward South Africa

What Comes Next?

People naturally try to understand the unfamiliar in terms of the familiar. Many Americans perceive the racial conflict in South Africa in terms of their own civil rights struggle. That perception is dangerously misleading.[1]

—Bobby Godsell

After years of scant notice, South Africa now seems regularly (almost cyclically) to emerge as a U.S. foreign policy issue. U.S. policy toward South Africa has attracted attention from a wide-range of American political, business and religious activists, all supporting or advancing their particular platforms. As on many controversial foreign policy issues, there is a domestic policy perspective which defines some of the motives and actions of the various players. As Bobby Godsell, a labor expert with Anglo American, and others have observed, the U.S. civil rights movement frequently is the starting point for many Americans attempting to understand the South African equation. To be sure, the desire for racial justice is most commendable. However, the similarities between Selma and Soweto are few. What an American perspective can offer, however, is the understanding that racial equality can lead to social harmony and guarantee freedom and liberties for individuals.

The question that must determine any U.S. government policy or initiative toward South Africa is simply this: Does it bolster the democratic middle ground? The U.S. Secretary of State's Advisory Committee on South Africa stated American's concern for South Africa when it wrote,

> The U.S. cannot stand aside as a human tragedy of potentially immense proportions threatens to unfold in South Africa. The stakes are too high. At risk are the lives of thousands, possibly millions, of South Africans, black and white, the future political and economic viability of the entire southern third of the African continent, and history's judgment of the United States.[2]

Yet the United States must face a complex set of foreign policy concerns; having been lured into a grave situation it has found its power and influence quite limited. Helen Kitchen, a renowned Africanist, wrote in 1984 that

> the U.S. has only limited ability to influence developments in South Africa. Particularly in the short run, we do not possess any levers that can be used to force the white ruling group to move faster or further than its own assessment of risks and gains dictates or to leverage blacks to adjust their priorities and tactics to our perceptions. . . . We can educate, prod, cajole, encourage, bolster; we cannot coerce, compel, or force change in what drives the components of this most complex society to their uncertain destiny.[3]

Caught between an unwillingness to sit by and watch the possible destruction of a nation and the inability of the U.S. government to force a solution, Washington's foreign policy must identify the areas where it can assist and complement the democratic elements that exist within South Africa today. Such a policy must focus on three basic platforms:

1. opposition to apartheid;
2. resistance to Marxist-oriented armed revolution;
3. assistance to all economic, political and cultural efforts that lead toward a constitutional democracy.

Within this broad outline of goals the U.S. government has essentially four different strategy options that it may follow:

1. Alliance and friendship with the Pretoria regime. This option has not been plausible for some time. Apartheid legislation, although rapidly changing, is still the law of the land and the South

African government's official policy. The U.S. goal of ending apartheid cannot be reconciled with this strategy.

2. Military intervention. Although a few U. S. politicians have made reference to this possibility, it is not a realistic option. Other countries, however, are willing to get involved militarily. The Soviet Union continues to train and arm the ANC's military wing.

3. Democratic enhancement. This strategy would attempt to engage tactics and parties that can bring about the destruction of apartheid while laying the foundation for a fully democratic South Africa. It concentrates on the democratic middle ground, yet recognizes the importance of both the existing regime and its pretenders in Lusaka. Carrots and sticks are applied not only to Pretoria, but also to all parties within the equation.

4. Ostracism. All U.S. contacts, within both the public and private sectors, would be reduced or eliminated. U.S. isolation from the affairs and outcomes in South Africa would invariably result.

The U.S. foreign policy debate over South Africa clearly centers on the last two strategies. The U.S. government's position has undergone a steady shift towards ostracism. The Comprehensive Anti-Apartheid Act (CAAA) of 1986 clearly moved the official U.S. policy to a more isolationist position. Given the assumption that the U.S. government's goal ought to be to bolster the democrats, the question to be addressed is how Washington can alter its current course—from neo-isolation to one which effectively undergirds the middle ground.

Sending a Message

The rationale for many diplomatic and foreign policy initiatives is to deliver a message. In South Africa's case, the first message that needs to be sent to all South Africans is that the U.S. firmly opposes apartheid and supports the establishment of full democracy. It is not enough to condemn apartheid; it is also necessary to formulate clear-headed policies capable of assisting in ending it, bearing in mind the limited leverage which is available.

A strategy of ostracism is reflected in the Comprehensive Anti-Apartheid Act of 1986. The sanctions legislation was a conspicuous signal to Pretoria and the world: the U.S. was willing to express its hatred for apartheid in economic terms. As a clear message the isolation tactic rings loudest. But for delivering results that assist the South African middle ground in its fight to destroy apartheid and build democracy, sanctions legislation can do more harm than good. Cutting off trade, reducing capital investment, discouraging corporate involvement and encouraging disinvestment are all tactics of isolation. They all generate signals, but once that message has been sent and received, the relationship is finished; another signal cannot be sent because there is no longer a medium through which to deliver it.

A policy of democratic enhancement, on the other hand, sends signals that are not as flashy but which sustain a medium that enables additional messages to travel in both directions. This is not to suggest that U.S. foreign policy decisions should be based solely on pursuing dialogue, no matter what the cost. Such a tactic would inevitably encourage appeasement when confrontation might sometimes be the appropriate tactic. But the type of isolation that has been encouraged by the CAAA will ultimately undermine the democratic middle ground in South Africa, the very element that the U.S. ought to be aiding. To assist those pursuing a just, post-apartheid nation, most economic channels must remain open. For it is within the economy that apartheid has failed; that failure must be exploited.

Another element that must be considered in trying to "send a message" is the peculiar psychology of the Afrikaner government. Like other authoritarian ruling parties, the regime perceives messages in a rather distorted context. Many in Pretoria read the sanctions bill—whatever the intentions of its framers—as a message that nothing further their government could do, short of immediately handing over the keys to their enemies, would please the U.S. Congress. A strategy of ostracism will always run the risk of such misperceptions, and when isolation has been achieved, there is no avenue for clarification, revision or cooperation.

A final factor in sending appropriate messages is timing. Bobby Godsell writes, "Strategies for change in South Africa need to be framed in terms of years, perhaps even decades."[4] This is anathema to many U.S. policy-makers. Americans are short-term, task-oriented workers; patience, particularly in international affairs, is not our long suit. A quick, clear signal, such as the imposition of economic sanctions, is the mode in which we prefer to work. During Senate hearings leading up to the CAAA, one senator predicted that if the Senate passed the sanctions legislation, then the Pretoria government would, within days or weeks, release Nelson Mandela.[5]

Such short-term strategies, with the expectation of quick results, lend themselves to following a policy of isolation rather than engagement. Democratic enhancement requires an appreciation for the long term, for it is only over the longer time frame that authentic, democratic change will occur in South Africa.

Economic Carrots and Sticks
(or Radishes and Twigs)

The impact of economic sanctions upon a given nation is inversely related to the degree of diversification of that country's economic base and its international trading links. If, like South Africa, the country is reasonably diversified in its manufacturing and service sectors, then it can rapidly develop indigenous substitutes for any products that may be embargoed. South Africa proved this capability when, in the 1960s and 1970s, a global arms embargo forced it to become self-sufficient in weapons and ammunition. Other embargoes of products ranging from industrial explosives (used in the mines) to petroleum, have resulted in South African industrial adaptation and successful substitution. The effectiveness of economic sanctions is also diminished when a nation such as South Africa has multiple trading partners, some of which do not adhere to or enforce various sanctions. The South African economy, traditionally based on trade with Europe and North America, has recently greatly expanded its export markets and its import sources to include countries in the Middle East, Asia, South America and the Pacific. One economic sanction that can have a large impact, particularly on a semi-developed nation, is the cutoff of foreign capital. The South African economy is not large enough to provide the capital necessary to fuel any significant long-term growth. Currently, U.S. capital sources have dried up (under the CAAA of 1986 it is illegal for U.S. financial institutions to make new loans to South Africa). European and Far Eastern sources, however, have been quietly filling some of the gap, making available some short-term money. The "alternative recommendations" of the U.S. Secretary of State's Advisory Committee's Report on South Africa are absolutely correct in stating, "Intensified sanctions, whether unilateral or multilateral, cannot serve as the cornerstone of a policy aimed at positive and creative goals. . . ."[6]

When assessing the possibilities of increased sanctions, U.S. legislators and policy-makers must consider what impact the current sanctions have had on achieving the United States' goals. Even with a diversified economic base and a variety of trading partners, economic sanctions do have a draining effect on an economy. But rather than destroying or seriously crippling the South African economy, sanctions like those the U.S. Congress imposed merely stunt economic growth. Such sanctions do their work so slowly that it allows the politicians plenty of time to adjust, hence the political pressure is minimal. The "stick" of sanctions is beginning to look more like a "twig."

The economic and political evidence suggests that it is within a growing, not static or shrinking, economy that South Africa has the greatest likelihood of creating a new, more just structure. The significant reforms that have occurred have come during prosperous times; an expanding economy works against apartheid. The soft "underbelly" of apartheid is a growing South African economy; the U.S. must bolster that economy and assist, rather than restrain, any growth potential. Rather than encouraging and assisting South Africa's economy to grow, the U.S. government has recently acted as a major obstacle to furthering trade or investment links with South Africa, thus hindering growth.

The repercussions of the Anti-Apartheid Act are beginning to be identified both in South Africa and in the United States. The agricultural and coal mining sectors of the South African economy have been hit particularly hard by sanctions, resulting in thousands of lost jobs—jobs primarily held by blacks. Accordingly, there has been a significant backlash within the South African black community concerning the sanctions issue; some black workers are pointing fingers at sanctions advocates as the source of their joblessness.[7]

In the United States, Paul Freedenburg, then Assistant Secretary of Commerce, reported in a House Foreign Affairs Committee hearing that 40 percent of the time and energy of Commerce's import control division has been spent on looking for and checking South African imports.[8] The sanctions measures are affecting not only the South African employment situation; they are also costing the U.S. citizen.

According to one econometric study, U.S. coal exporters lost $250 million in 1986 and 1987 due to the 1986 Comprehensive Anti-Apartheid Act. This, in turn, resulted in the loss of between 3,000 to 7,000 U.S. coal-mining jobs.[9] In New Jersey, where the state passed disinvestment laws, the New Jersey state pension fund had reduced earnings of more than $360 million between 1985 and 1986.[10] (It is striking that the cost of sanctions to the U.S. economy far exceeds America's total foreign aid budget for all of Africa, $941.9 million for 1988.)[11]

The Anti-Apartheid Act of 1986, however ineffective in producing the U.S. government's goals in South Africa, is in place and must be used in as positive a fashion as possible. The "stick" (or perhaps twig) of sanctions has been applied—now the lifting of sanctions must be used as an effective carrot. Section-by-section, the act could be suspended if the Pretoria regime enacted specific legislation. When and if the Group Areas Act is repealed, for instance, the ban on agricultural products could be lifted. The U.S. could hold out the possibility that other sections within the CAAA might be lifted if Nelson Mandela were released and the ANC and other organizations unbanned. The strategy would hold that each step toward dismantling apartheid would be reinforced with a positive act that would bolster the South African economy. Singing rhetorical praises of the Pretoria regime is unnecessary and wrong, given its highly questionable moral legitimacy, but a quid pro quo that would result in bolstering the South African economy assists the middle ground in its fight for a post-apartheid democracy and provides for at least some U.S. leverage on the situation. This kind of flexible and energetic initiative would have to be a combined executive and legislative branch effort if it were to succeed.

The Anti-Apartheid Act explicitly states,

> The Congress hereby urges the U.S. government to assist in all appropriate ways the realization by South African blacks and other non-whites of their rightful place in the South African economy.

The U.S. government must be faithful to this mandate and

initiate specific economic programs that will bolster the democratic middle ground. Black business development is central to exploiting the failures of apartheid. U.S. government assistance and aid should be targeted for black-owned and operated South African firms. U.S. corporations that remain in South Africa should receive cooperation and encouragement from the U.S. government as they subscribe to and adhere to fair labor practices such as the Sullivan Principles. (Private sector initiatives will be discussed in the next chapter.)

The U.S. government can act as a clearinghouse or coordinator for black South Africans who are seeking higher education and training. U.S. AID funds ($26 million in fiscal year 1986 and approximately $27 million in fiscal year 1987) have been earmarked for various black activist projects, in accordance with the Anti-Apartheid Act. (The general language of the legislation calls for assistance to "the victims of apartheid.") This AID funding should concentrate on formal education for black students, black economic empowerment and health care and training.

There are a variety of projects and programs that can be initiated by the U.S. government in its effort to assist South Africa's democrats in overcoming the polarization of their society and building a foundation for a free nation. In the economic realm, the U.S. government has a role to play, particularly with regard to trade and investment legislation. The quick fix temptation of increased sanctions is an allurement U.S. foreign policy-makers must resist. Washington needs to constantly remind itself of its long-term goals for South Africa, avoiding any further isolation which would diminish the middle ground.

The Negotiating Table:
Who Is Invited and How Can We Help?

The legislative and executive branches of the U.S. government must support the formation of a positive environment for negotiations between the Pretoria government and black leaders. This would entail conveying to all parties the long-term (and short-term) benefits of beginning negotiations. Some highly significant discussions between authentic leaders have already begun—the Indaba and the Soweto rent boycott and electricity negotiations being the most productive and concrete examples. U.S. foreign policy-makers must recognize the importance of the negotiations that have already occurred and support those that are still embryonic.

In its creation of a favorable climate for negotiations, the U.S. government must recognize who the key players are and who should be encouraged (or pressed) to join the negotiating process. The South African government, morally illegitimate as it may be, is the de facto ruling party. The ANC, as repugnant as some of its violent, revolutionary tactics may be, continues to command an important degree of influence within South Africa. Other groups are also critically important, including the trade unions, Inkatha, the UDF, municipal and homeland leaders, and Indian and coloured groups. All parties should be encouraged and persuaded by U.S. officials to enter into negotiations. To influence these various groups, the U.S. government must have contact and relations with their leadership. Some groups will respond more readily than others to U.S. persuasion; the United States currently has varying degrees of leverage with the different organizations.

In early 1987 the U.S. State Department sent the U.S. Congress a briefing paper on South Africa. Part of the research and discussion focused on the character of the ANC. One of the conclusions suggested that ". . . if ANC relations with Western countries continue to improve, serious policy differences could surface within the ANC."[12] The implication is that the ANC might experience some type of split if the West (and Pretoria) could apply the correct pressure. That schism, the theory goes, would allow the "nationalist" element within the ANC to break away from the "communist" faction—the nationalists being more likely to enter into negotiations. Such a split, however, may not occur for some time. As Tom Lodge suggests,

> Any split within the ANC between Marxists and nationalists is not plausible. It is too crude to view the ANC as divided between Marxists and nationalists; there are gradations between the two. The two strains are built into the history of the ANC's own development. These aren't sort of recent overlays that can be shunned off at will.[13]

The U.S. government needs to recognize this dilemma. This is not to suggest that the ANC should be excluded from talks or kept in isolation—just the opposite. A democratic enhancement policy should mean involvement with all parties, particularly the ANC.

The ANC elite should be given the opportunity to express its views and goals for a post-apartheid South Africa. The opportunity for the ANC leadership to drift away from its Marxist orientation and shed its communist influence should always be made available.

The Role of Mediator

It is probably the quintessential dream of every U.S. diplomat ever involved with southern Africa to be a "mediator" between the parties negotiating a new South Africa. It is not an unrealistic dream. In fact, it is quite plausible and honorable and should be encouraged. As the Anglican bishop of Durban, Michael Nuttal, stated,

> In the long run we're going to need the U.S. and the West to help sort out our dilemma. We'll need wise and compassionate people without axes to grind, coming in to assist us in the negotiating process and in the aftermath, the implementation of the negotiations.[14]

The U.S. government could offer to provide communication and logistical services for any negotiating sessions. Afrikaners cannot "go home" to work out an agreement, and they certainly do not look to the Netherlands as a potential mediator. The United Kingdom, particularly under Prime Minister Margaret Thatcher, and the U.S. appear to be the most likely to play a significant role. The United States' recent role in the Angolan-Namibian peace settlement provides a base of familiarity and possibly a certain degree of trust that could go a long way in allowing the U.S. to become actively involved in a South African negotiation process. The British, with their historical, economic and cultural ties with South Africa, are also well-poised to assist such a process. The Thatcher government is highly respected and closely listened to in Pretoria. (Many in the opposition movement, particularly in the ANC, perceive Thatcher as a crony and ally of Pretoria.) As in any negotiating process, language becomes critical. Any reference to a "Lancaster House-type agreement" (perceived by many in South Africa as an agreement mandated by outside international forces, as occurred in Rhodesia) sends up large red flags for many in Pretoria—a mistake that has been made by the Eminent Persons Group and others.

If the middle ground in South Africa can persevere, there will come a day when all parties will recognize the need and demonstrate the necessary willingness to enter into negotiations. When that time arrives the United States can assist in bridging the chasm of suspicion that will undoubtedly separate the participants. Being tapped for such a role will come about only if the American government can demonstrate an honest and unbiased policy. This does not mean following a unprincipled path, being credulously accommodating to all parties. The U.S. government's firm and total commitment to a post-apartheid, multi-party democratic system is the key component for a role as mediator, in winning the respect of all groups striving to achieve these ends.

Indaba

The U.S. role as a mediator in negotiations is a worthy long-term vision, though it may well take years or even decades to come to fruition. In the short-term, however, there are actions the U.S. government can take to sustain the middle ground's negotiating efforts. The Indaba demonstrates the ability of South Africans, of all races and creeds, to sit down together and produce a realistic proposal for a non-racial, second-tier government. Dr. Oscar Dhlomo, a co-convener of the Indaba, has urged the U.S. government to lend support publicly to the Indaba process.

If the U.S. government would give credibility and support to negotiations like the Indaba, which thus far they don't appear to be doing too much of, then it would strengthen the middle ground.[15]

Specifically, there are a number of programs that Washington could adopt to bolster the Indaba, pressure Pretoria into looking favorably upon it, and encourage other negotiating sessions throughout South Africa. The U.S. government should provide incentives for the implementation of the Indaba's proposals, including:

• offer to underwrite substantial development assistance to the KwaZulu-Natal (Kwa-Natal) province. (This aid could include money for education, housing and agriculture, among other programs.)

• offer to lift sanctions restrictions on Kwa-Natal commodities and products. These would include agricultural commodities grown and processed in the region, such as sugar, as well as minerals, such as coal.

• offer technical support and assistance in establishing free trade zones throughout Kwa-Natal and consider any goods manufactured in the zones to be qualified for GSP (Generalized System of Preferences) tariffs. (The U.S. government might want to allow all manufactured products from Kwa-Natal to be qualified for GSP.)

• encourage and assist American venture capital to flow to projects and companies in Kwa-Natal. (Under the Anti-Apartheid Act, U.S. investment is allowed only if it is going to a black-owned company. Unfortunately, this exception has not been publicized, so few black-owned companies have taken advantage of it.) All U.S. investment would be legalized for Kwa-Natal companies.

The benefits that such programs would produce for the Indaba, Kwa-Natal and all of South Africa far outweigh the liabilities. The people of the Kwa-Natal region would directly benefit from electing to pursue a more just, democratic system. South Africans, black and white, from the other provinces would be able to see the tangible benefits of pursuing negotiations and political compromise. Such results could well encourage them to press on with their own existing negotiations or initiate new ones. If the United States were to demonstrate significant support, both financial and political, for a second-tier project such as the Indaba, it would send authentic signals about what Washington would be willing to do for a national constitutional discussion. Black and white elites need to be prodded and pushed toward talking. When the U.S. government lines up squarely behind a democratic compromise such as the Indaba, it exhibits America's commitment to negotiations for a post-apartheid South Africa.

U.S. foreign policy toward South Africa, shaped by a mixture of domestic as well as international factors, must adhere to one basic principle, that of assisting the liberal, democratic middle ground of South Africa struggling to deliver a post-apartheid nation founded on individual liberties. Currently the U.S. government is drifting toward a neo-isolationist policy, a move exemplified by the Comprehensive Anti-Apartheid Act of 1986. Washington ought to halt this trend and embark upon a new course of democratic enhancement.

This is not to suggest that the U.S. government can single-handedly bring an end to apartheid and create a new dispensation. All external players must recognize that foreign pressure is less of a force for change than internal democratic organizations. Outside pressure should be couched in terms of strengthening black empowerment groups inside South Africa, not attempting to act as a substitute for them. The U.S. government needs to be involved in sending a message, offering economic incentives and penalties and assisting any authentic negotiating efforts. All programs and initiators must be motivated by (1) the elimination of apartheid; (2) the resistance to armed revolution; and (3) assistance in the establishment of a multi-party, democratic system which guarantees individual rights and freedoms. This is not to suggest that the U.S. government can single-handedly bring an end to apartheid and create a new dispensation. All external players must recognize that foreign pressure is less of a force for change than internal democratic organizations. Outside pressure should be couched in terms of strengthening black empowerment groups inside South Africa, not attempting to act as a substitute for them.

The U.S. government must recognize that "sending messages" should not translate into moralistic rhetoric which ostracizes key players. The appropriate message is one which demonstrates America's willingness to support, materially and morally, those South Africans who are pursuing the "third option" —one which rejects the authoritarian policies of apartheid and the totalitarian visions of revolutionary movements.

The economy remains the primary medium for the erosion of apartheid. Black political power will continue to increase due to the economic leverage the black community is gaining. Washington needs to encourage black economic empowerment by assisting black-owned and black-managed businesses. The U.S. government needs to encourage American firms in South Africa to remain and continue their fair labor practices, which have become increasingly emulated by South African-owned corporations. Increased sanctions will do nothing but accentuate the isolationist trend, undermining a primary tool of the democratic middle ground. Promoting negotiations between all parties should always be a primary tenet of U.S. policy toward South Africa.

The long-term strategy must be one of helping to build an environment for authentic talks. Washington must have contact with all willing parties, no matter what their political or ideological stripe. A realistic assessment of each of the potential negotiating parties becomes essential if we are to be useful mediators between hostile groups.

Maintaining a balanced approach requires the total commitment to a post-apartheid, multi-party democracy that guarantees individual liberties. If the U.S. government explicitly enunciates such a position from the beginning, all parties will respect and understand our motivations. Those groups unwilling to work for these commitments and goals might reject the United States as mediator; it is a risk worth taking in our pursuit of assisting the South African middle ground.

From a short-term perspective the United States can lend its support to existing negotiating forums and proposals such as the Indaba. Various legislative and executive actions could be taken in Washington to help the Indaba proposals become reality.

As a nation and a government the United States has strategic, economic, political, humanitarian and moral interests in South Africa. Our government must avoid a course of isolation and embrace one of involvement. But the government is not the sole potential support for the democratic middle ground; the private sector also has a pivotal role to play.

Twelve

The U. S. Private Sector
Sending Help and Setting Examples for the Democratic Middle Ground

The real tragedy of South Africa is that Christians around the world are just watching it slip into revolution.[1]

—Nana Mahomo

Americans concerned about South Africa, both individually and corporately, ask what they can do to help a struggling nation give birth to a new order. Numerous avenues exist for all Westerners to assist in bolstering the middle ground's goal of a more free, more just and democratic country. But superimposed on these strategies and tactics must be a commitment—not unlike that which the true liberals in South Africa must make. Americans, like their democratic brothers and sisters in South Africa, must be willing to stand up to the polarized and radicalized perspectives and policies that have emerged in the South African debate. As Americans we witness this polarizing process from a safe distance; South Africans, however, are having it played out in their daily lives. But like the democrats in South Africa, we must be willing to criticize or applaud actions which inhibit or encourage South

Africa's journey to democracy. When the Pretoria regime detains hundreds of children without charges we must demand their release. When the ANC plants bombs which indiscriminately maim and kill, we must condemn that act for what it is: terrorism. In the United States we must avoid and expose the increasingly popular divisive policy that demands "choosing sides" between two unacceptable alternatives.

Many in the U.S. anti-apartheid movement have openly embraced violent tactics. The not-so-subtle implication is: if you do not support the armed revolution, then you must favor apartheid. That is precisely the polarizing technique used in South Africa by radicals, and it must be resisted by all Americans who recognize that there is a third option—a middle ground that seeks democratic values guaranteed by individual freedoms. As in most scenarios that entail radical divisiveness, the middle ground—the reconcilers—is often implicitly and explicitly criticized. One American clergyman described South African blacks who do not subscribe to certain radical tactics as "quislings."[2]

As liberals, democrats and Christians, we must stand up to the polarizers. And we must accept the likelihood that in resisting their destructive approach to South Africa, we too will become an objects of their wrath. Actual strategies and tactics for assisting the South African middle ground must emerge from the imagination and commitment of concerned Americans. Like the public sector, U.S. private institutions must recognize that their influence is clearly limited. Outsiders can help, but South Africans themselves hold the ultimate solutions. A policy of democratic enhancement for the private sector means providing assistance and demonstrating policies that encourage the middle ground as it pursues its goals. The business community, trade unions, churches and a wide variety of educational institutions (including the press) can provide such opportunities.

The Corporate Connection

American companies have been doing business in and with South Africa since the last century. These companies can assist the middle ground through their example of management, their provision of venture capital and their educational abilities. To keep this American influence in perspective, however, it must be remembered that South Africa represents less than one percent of U.S. foreign trade and less than one percent of U.S. direct investment overseas.[3] U.S. investment in South Africa represents about 14 percent of South Africa's total foreign investment and generates two percent of the South African GNP.[4]

Setting a corporate example for two decades has been, and should continue to be, a critical task for U.S. companies to shoulder. Even when announcing that he was giving up his own corporate guidelines, the Reverend Leon Sullivan proudly stated,

> The (Sullivan) Principles have caused a revolution in industrial race relations in South Africa and have broken new ground for black workers in South Africa that has not existed for three hundred years.[5]

The Sullivan Principles not only provide a code for U.S corporations to follow, but more importantly they also set a working example for all South African companies to emulate. Sal Marzullo, Chairman of the Industry Support Unit to the Sullivan Statement of Principles, stated,

> U.S. company efforts (in South Africa) have helped galvanize thinking on the need for change among other institutions in the country . . . (U.S. corporate) efforts are multiplied by those of leading South African businessmen who have publicly committed themselves to a full and equal role for blacks in both the economic and political life of South Africa.[6]

Leon Sullivan was asked in December 1986, six months prior to his call for total U.S. divestment, who would replace the U.S. companies at the cutting edge of labor reform when and if they withdraw from South Africa. He took a long pause and answered, "I do not know and that worries me."[7]

Since 1977 the Sullivan Principles have contributed to what John Kane-Berman has called "creative erosion." The foreign business community is, and will continue to be, an important link in eroding apartheid. U.S. companies are helping to destroy apartheid when they assist black employees who wish to move out of black townships and into white areas or when they provide legal assistance to their black workers (as General Motors did), "testing" the boundaries of racial segregation. Mr. Rudolph Agnew, chairman of the British firm Consolidated Gold Fields, described the corporate sector's role in these terms:

> Foreign companies with interests in South Africa can go further than they have and push and test apartheid laws. There is, however, a danger that all corporations must be aware of, and that is the problem of being patronizing. What white South Africa needs to do is break out of this attitude, and U.S. and British companies can assist. The mining companies, for instance, must let the black workers decide what type of housing structure they want to live in. The key is that South Africa needs to rid itself of this old patronizing attitude, and if it can, everyone benefits.[8]

Mr. Agnew's point ought to be heeded. In their pursuit of assisting black entrepreneurship and increasing the level of black management, U.S. companies must not fall into the old South African trap of white patronage—a policy that inevitably produces dependence rather than independence.

Foreign businesses in South Africa are in positions to demonstrate effectively their political and economic concerns to the Pretoria government. British Petroleum's plan (see chapter 10) to construct a R100 million multi-racial town is an example of a foreign company's potential impact. Many U.S. companies commit large percentages of dividends or profits produced from their South African operations to the communities in which they operate. Union Carbide, for instance, uses 100 percent of the dividends from its South African operations—amounting to $1-2 million per annum—to assist black workers in education, housing improvements and legal aid.[9] In 1984 to 1986 U.S. companies in South Africa spent $150 million on social programs alone. Housing, education, management and industrial training are critical areas where U.S. companies can continue to make significant contributions.

One of the greatest needs that has emerged in recent years is for venture capital to underwrite black entrepreneurs. Black businesses have access to only limited amounts of capital from South African sources. Although South African banks and building societies (savings and loans) have recently devoted greater percentages of their portfolios to black-owned companies, there is a very large demand that is not being filled domestically. Foreign capital is essential if the black business community is to grow. U.S. corporations already in South Africa can provide some of that needed capital in the form of loans, equipment or direct equity investment. Capital from U.S. companies or investors not currently in South Africa must also be encouraged. The Comprehensive Anti-Apartheid Act of 1986 allows for U.S. individuals or groups to invest in South African companies if they are black-owned. (The Treasury Department has yet to define "black-owned.") Along with helping to start black-owned and black-managed companies, the U.S. corporate sector needs to assist blacks in purchasing existing white-owned companies. Sam Motsuenjane, former President of the black South African chamber of commerce, believes black ownership in traditionally white companies is essential.

> Special venture capital funds must be created to enable blacks to acquire shareholding in white-owned companies, either via the Stock Ex-change or privately.[10]

(Unfortunately current U.S. law prohibits any venture capital going to future black shareholders if the company in which they invest is owned by whites.)

It would be particularly beneficial if U.S. companies and investors would link their available capital to certain political developments. For instance, U.S. companies could promise to invest in Kwa-Natal if the Indaba proposals are implemented. (This would have to be coordinated with a congressional action. The Anti-Apartheid Act would have to be amended to lift legal restrictions on any new investment.) U.S. corporations could follow the example of British Petroleum, conditioning new development plans on the removal of certain apartheid legislation. This approach would require the cooperation of the Pretorian regime, the U.S. government and the private sector to make strides in not only economically bolstering the middle ground but also in laying the groundwork for future negotiating channels.

U.S. corporate influence must be aimed at all sectors of the South African society and power structure, ranging from government officials in Pretoria to the black entrepreneur in Durban to the exiled revolutionary elite in Lusaka or Dar es Salaam. The U.S. corporate community probably carries little weight with ANC leaders; nevertheless, the ANC elite represents a group of influential politicians and military men who will most likely have a say in South Africa's future. Attempting to demonstrate to the ANC leadership the viability of a free market economy is a worthwhile endeavor. Those revolutionaries whose first priority really is economic justice might be affected by historical examples of successful and failed economic systems.

In May 1987 the Business International Conference met in London to discuss the "Strategic Options for International Companies" in South Africa. Oliver Tambo was one of the four speakers, along with David Willers of the South Africa Foundation, Sir Leslie Smith of the British Industrial Council of South Africa and John Kane-Berman of the South African Institute on Race Relations. Such conferences and dialogues must be applauded and encouraged in the future. Perhaps one such meeting could focus on the successes and failures of various economic models, particularly in Africa, with participants including African and East European leaders who have opted for partially-free market systems. Unfortunately many of the trained economists within the ANC are Marxists, and their economic discussions are prone to rely heavily upon political and ideological rhetoric. Nevertheless, such discussions have the potential of demonstrating economic realities to the less doctrinaire revolutionaries.

All of these tactics and programs require a commitment on the part of U.S. companies to remain active and involved in South Africa. Divestment and withdrawal does little to assist free-market trends in the South African economic arena. The leverage factor is obvious; once an American corporation sells or closes its operations, its involvement and influence is radically reduced or eliminated.

Labor Unions

Like the corporate community, U.S. trade unions have valuable opportunities to encourage and enhance the middle ground's objectives. Legalized in 1979, the black trade union movement has been a leading factor in black economic power and increasing political leverage. COSATU, the largest union federation, now claims more than 800,000 members, including some 25 different unions. The second largest union federation, the National Council of Trade Unions (NACTU), has more than 300,000 members.

Links between American and South African trade unions date back to the 1950s and 1960s. As black unions began to emerge in the 1960s and 1970s, at first without the recognition of Pretoria, the U.S. labor unions initiated contact and assistance. The AFL-

CIO has officially recognized COSATU (formed in 1985) and NACTU (formed by the AZACTU-CUSA merger in 1987). The AFL-CIO does not have ties with UWUSA, a labor union associated with Inkatha. The American labor unions continue to support the South African unions with educational funding as well as technical and consultative assistance on labor organization. It is hoped that this very positive relationship between U.S. and South African unions will facilitate a moderating influence upon the increasingly radical COSATU leadership.

In recent years COSATU's demands steadily radicalized from the traditional (Western) objectives of better wages and working conditions to a call for revolution. A July 1987 COSATU convention strongly reflected this increase in political activity. Elijah Barayi, President of COSATU, stated, "Politics . . . is a bread and butter issue for the working class."[11] Particularly, in a militant speech that demonstrated COSATU's rapid politicization, he warned that unionists would lead the revolutionary overthrow of the government. "This intransigent government will not hand over power. The black majority shall have to seize power."[12]

It is difficult to measure the radicalization and politicization of COSATU's rank and file, but it is becoming apparent that the union leadership is adopting increasingly radical rhetoric.

The union leadership has frequently set the tone at conventions and meetings by encouraged ovations from the floor when "fraternal greetings" are received from the South African Communist Party.[13]

Fortunately not all trade union leaders are driven by anti-capitalist sentiments. Phiroshaw Camay, head of NACTU, plainly stated,

> We must ensure that the post-apartheid unions are free, independent and democratic. We don't want to become transmission belts of a one-party state.[14]

U.S. trade unions need to reinforce the democratic elements, such as Camay and others, within the union movement. The importance of strong labor unions in South Africa, both for economic and democratic reasons, cannot be underestimated. The task of the American unionists must be to focus on encouraging the middle ground and to help union leaders refrain from taking part in the polarization process. Although the National Union of

Mineworkers' Strike in 1987 greatly increased tensions, labor union/management relations in South Africa have been one of the best models of genuine black/white power sharing. Now this relationship, like much of South African society, is being thrown into a political centrifuge—pushing everything to extremes. U.S. trade unions have an opportunity to provide services and funding which encourage the development of the middle ground and resist the radicalization now emerging within the South African labor movement.

U. S. Churches and the Middle Ground

As Nana Mahomo of the African-American Labor Institute said, "The real tragedy of South Africa is that Christians around the world are just watching it slip into revolution." U.S. churches can play vital roles encouraging the third option to become the dominant strategy within South Africa. Both spiritually and materially, American Christians can support their South African brothers and sisters in their effort to establish a new social and political structure. Unfortunately many mainline U.S. denominations do not appear to be as supportive of the middle ground as they could be. In fact, they are not watching South Africa "slip into revolution"; they seem to be actively "pushing" it towards the revolutionary brink.

Since the mid-1970s U.S. churches have targeted South Africa as one of their key foreign policy concerns. It is, of course, important that American churches express solidarity with their brothers and sisters living under the injustice of apartheid. Few U.S. Christians dispute the goal of eliminating apartheid. However, there are significant differences over how best to end apartheid while at the same time ensuring a post-apartheid democratic state. Mainline church leaders seem all too willing to trust those whose commitment to democratic values is in grave doubt.

In December 1985 a delegation of American church leaders attended the "Harare Consultation"—a World Council of Churches "emergency meeting" designed to "inform" international church leaders on church developments in South Africa. At the Harare meeting the "Kairos Document" was embraced and adopted. The U.S. church representatives who attended the WCC meeting pledged that they would implement the Harare Declaration, which called for 1) actions to prevent the extension of loans to any South African bank, corporation or government-affiliated institution; 2) application of "immediate and comprehensive" economic sanctions against South Africa; 3) support for "South African movements working for the liberation of their country."[15] To carry out their directions, the leaders formed the Churches' Emergency Committee on Southern Africa (CECSA).

The rhetoric used by U.S. church leaders in their call for the formation of CECSA is most revealing:

• United Methodist Bishop James Ault, repeating slogans from the Kairos Document, said, "Enough is enough. Time is up for South Africa. The moment of truth (Kairos) is now."[16]

• Reverend Avery Post, President of the United Church of Christ, delivered his verdict: "The moment has come for liberation rather than reformation. "[17]

• Reverend M. Lorenzo Shepard, President of the Progressive National Baptist Church, dismissed any South African blacks opposed to economic sanctions:"There will always be quislings in any liberation movement."[18]

With the formation of CECSA, the mainline church leaders christened 1986 as "the year of action by U.S. churches against apartheid." The Emergency Committee immediately committed itself to the drive for stringent economic sanctions against South Africa. On June 16, 1986, the Reverend Avery Post opened the Washington, D.C., CECSA meeting by calling the Reagan Administration and its policy toward South Africa "bankrupt" and "morally empty." The purpose of the Capitol Hill meeting was clearly to champion economic sanctions. U.S. Representative Ron Dellums (D-CA) called on the church leaders to support his amendment (H.R. 997) to the more moderate "Anti-Apartheid Act" (H.R. 4868). The religious leaders enthusiastically supported Dellums' amendment which effectively called for an end to all U.S. business involvement in South Africa. Representative Dellums insisted that church leaders could be effective lobbyists. "You should not walk the halls of Congress as missionaries but go aggressively with a point of view," he counseled.[19] That point of view, of course, was to support vigorously Dellums' ban on all investment and trade with Pretoria. A CECSA spokesman explained proudly, "We are holding fast to the Dellums bill."[20]

During the summer of 1986 the U.S. church world was at the forefront of the "anti-apartheid campaign," spearheading the drive for the most comprehensive economic sanctions possible. American church leaders, however, were not in complete agreement on how best to approach the South African dilemma. While Dr. Benjamin Chavis, executive director of the United Church of Christ's Commission for Racial Justice, was typical in his demand that President Reagan"reverse his policy of constructive terrorism" and "constructive support of apartheid and to cut all ties with South Africa,"[21] Episcopal Bishop John Walker, the influential black prelate from Washington, D.C., broke ranks by declaring his concern for the negative repercussions that comprehensive sanctions might produce. In his testimony to the Senate Foreign Relations Committee, Bishop Walker warned that

> in our desire to do something, we have failed to connect actions with outcome. Our agony over the plight of the black people of South Africa has often trapped us into taking actions that may be more pronounced in their symbolism than in their capacity to bring substantive changes.[22]

Bishop Walker was swimming directly against the church tide and its call for "total economic sanctions" when he explained the importance of a healthy South African economy.

> We must seek to . . . bring the chances of a transition in South Africa to a more realistic level, and also make the cost of such transition more bearable by the existing economic structures, so as not to destroy it but to harness its productive energies for the benefit of all South Africans.[23]

With the passage of the Comprehensive Anti-Apartheid Act of 1986 (PL99-440) in the fall of 1986, mainline church activists began focusing on non-legislative matters. In cooperation with the Interfaith Center on Corporate Responsibility (ICCR), CECSA sent a letter to 100 corporations demanding that they publicly announce before October 1, 1986, that they would commit to shutting down their South Africa operations by the end of the year. The letter, signed by the Reverend Avery Post and the Reverend Lorenzo Shepard, stated that

> virtually all leaders with an authentic mandate from the South African black community are unanimous in their support for

sanctions and corporate withdrawal as the only peaceful means remaining by which to pressure the white minority for change.[24]

Along with disinvestment efforts, consumer boycotts and shareholder resolutions, the U.S. church activists promoted divestment of stockholdings in corporations that had South African connections. From seminaries to pension funds, to church publishing companies and individual parishes, church organizations were prodded to clear their stock portfolios of any South African-related U.S. corporations. In September 1986 the National Conference of Catholic Bishops joined many of its mainline Protestant colleagues in urging all U.S. Roman Catholic dioceses to sell their stock in American corporations doing business in South Africa, or to attempt to persuade those companies voluntarily to withdraw from engagement there. Although the National Conference resolution was not binding, the recommendation brought significant pressure on most of the American Catholic dioceses, as well as Catholic colleges and universities, to oblige.

By the spring of 1987 it was becoming apparent that the punitive economic policies pushed by the churches had played into the hands of both reactionaries and radicals in South Africa. Legislative sanctions, disinvestment and divestiture helped push the Pretoria regime further into the laager, resulting in U.S. government and private sector influence hitting an all-time low. The South African black work force felt the sting of sanctions, as thousands of jobs, particularly in the agricultural and coal mining sector, were lost. Thanks to the implementation of sanctions, the whole of South African society continued to spin toward greater polarization.

For some in the church world, this result has been a great disappointment, and there may be a reassessment calling into question the wisdom of sanctions. For others, including Leon Sullivan, the hope remains that economic pressures will move Pretoria in a positive direction. For many mainline activists, however, aiding the violent revolutionary option has always been the ultimate goal.

Unfortunately certain patterns within the U.S. church world seem to be increasingly evident. Some American religious leaders supported economic sanctions against South Africa with the intention not of pressuring Pretoria into reform, but of destroying the South African economy and bolstering the armed struggle. Divestment and disinvestment efforts will no doubt continue; harsher and more punitive economic sanctions legislation will be drafted and promoted. In April 1988 various church groups, including the NCC, endorsed another round of sanctions legislation that would have effectively cut off all trade with South Africa and require U.S. corporations to disinvest within 12 months.

Shortly after the Lusaka Conference, the U.S. National Council of Churches (at its May 1987 Governing Board meeting) officially affirmed the Lusaka Statement, and efforts are currently underway to increase the U.S. Churches' contributions to the WCC's Special Fund to Combat Racism. The Special Fund, in turn, assists the ANC. A new religious group, initiated by the 18 U.S. Church representatives and anti-apartheid activists who attended the Lusaka Conference, was also formed in May 1987. "Campaign '88" was a national organization whose mission was to "assure that the issues of Southern Africa become a key issue for all candidates for election, especially for national office."[25]

Fortunately, this tendency of the mainline churches to encourage the polarization of South African society does not represent all of the U.S. churches' efforts in South Africa. There have been extremely helpful youth exchange programs sponsored by many U.S. denominations. Educational funds and youth travel programs are often mentioned by South African Christians as very tangible means for U.S. churches to assist South Africans. U.S. seminary training for South African clergy has also provided valuable assistance. Church-related groups, such as Africa Enterprise and the National Initiative for Reconciliation, also frequently look to the U.S. for funding.

On the parish level, there have been successful programs where one U.S. congregation "adopted" a South African church. The First Presbyterian Church of Lenoir, North Carolina, for instance, has provided funding directly to a black congregation in Kwa-Nubuhle Township near Uitenhage, enabling it to construct a permanent church building. Such parish-to-parish relationships should be encouraged and supported by the national church offices. (The risk to be avoided in such "adoptions" is the politicization of aid and assistance.)

Along with financial assistance, South African Christians gladly acknowledge their need for advice, criticism and example. Johan Heyns, Moderator of the Dutch Reformed Church, says,

We encourage the churches abroad to come up with criticisms of our new stance, the 1986 Synod statement (that apartheid cannot be biblically supported), which is only a beginning.[26]

Interaction between U.S. and South African churches can lead to a better understanding of our respective societies and a greater awareness of both theological and political perspectives.

American churches can offer assistance beyond the offering plate or theological dialogue. Michael Cassidy and other South African church leaders continually remind us that South Africa's needs are as much spiritual as material; the power of prayer cannot be minimized. Reconciliation contains elements of forgiveness and restitution, and neither can take place without spirit-filled guidance and intervention.

In their righteous indignation, many U.S. church leaders have called for increased sanctions against Pretoria or financial support for the armed revolution. These are hardly policies which bolster the middle ground. American Christians must call political decisions into question, but the real task of the U.S. churches lies well beyond declarations of support for specific congressional legislation. American churches have a spiritual responsibility in fostering and aiding the reconciliation process within South Africa. This is a task which cannot be accomplished if our involvement is unnecessarily divisive.

Education: A Two-Way Street

Quality education is essential in preparing black and white South Africans for leadership roles in a post-apartheid South Africa. The U.S. Secretary of State's Advisory Committee wrote,

While educational assistance will not provide quick political solutions, it can prepare young blacks to help administer and govern a future South Africa.[27]

Education is critical, particularly in the black communities where educational facilities and spending have been historically below the standards in white communities. (Functional illiteracy among blacks is more than 40 percent, and despite Pretoria's recent increases in allocations to black education, the ratio spent on white to black education is seven to one.) The U.S. private sector can actively assist in providing educational opportunities to South

Africa's youth. The need for qualified black teachers, for instance, is enormous. Funding for teacher education has come from U.S. corporations, church groups and educational institutions, but more will be required. In 1986 the Institute for International Education in New York established the South Africa Education Program Information Exchange which provides information concerning current South African educational needs.

Black education is in high demand in all areas and on all levels. And the U.S. private sector needs to assist in any way possible. Educational experts in South Africa, however, report a trend in black higher education that perhaps needs reshaping. On the university level, black students are focusing on the "soft subjects" rather than the more technical areas. Professor Gavin Maasdorp of Natal University suggests, "What South Africa is so in need of is black doctors, engineers, teachers, architects, business managers, and economists."[28] American universities should be encouraged to continue to expand their foreign exchange and scholarship programs for South African students, particularly in the sciences and more technically-oriented subjects.

American assistance to South African educational programs is an important element in a strategy of bolstering the middle ground. This is not to suggest that education is the cure-all, a role too frequently assigned to it. But education within a democratic environment is essential if South Africa is going to emerge with the "habits of the heart" suitable to a post-apartheid, democratic and free nation. Education requires years and decades. The U.S. private sector must aid the South African middle ground as it attempts to provide a political and economic climate that will allow for such a long-term project to be successful.

The reactionary Right and the revolutionary Left will undoubtedly continue to attempt to usurp the educational process and use it for their own ends. The polarization process is as evident in South Africa's educational system as anywhere else in the society. Whether calling it apartheid propaganda or "liberation education," the extremes use all levels of education to propagate their views and tactics. This activity in itself may not necessarily be detrimental if "the debate" can be heard in an objective, non-coercive forum. Unfortunately, such forums are the exception rather than the rule in South Africa today. U.S. educational assistance must recognize this polarizing trend and encourage more noncoercive, nonpolitical educational structures.

Education is indeed a two-way street, and educational programs, although differing in form and style, flow in all directions. Americans need to be more fully educated about the realities of South Africa. One of the American people's primary instructors on South Africa is the press. Currently, under the State of Emergency, the foreign press in South Africa is under restrictions which prohibit complete coverage of extraparliamentary political activities inside the country. All sectors of American society, both public and private, should encourage the Pretorian government to lift any and all press restrictions. Even with the press regulations, however, the Western media has been able to send valuable information concerning South African political, social and economic developments. Unfortunately, the U.S. media often tends to focus on the confrontational and violent aspects of the South African scene, rather than on the more subtle (and often more important) developments within the society. Accurate journalism (whether print, radio or television) demands an objectivity that is quite difficult to maintain, particularly within an increasingly politicized country such as South Africa.

Ignoring the significance of certain extraparliamentary groups, while overstating the importance of others, is the type of journalism that does a great disservice to the American reader and viewer. Accurate reporting will not only expose the U.S. public to the realities of South Africa, but it will, in fact, bolster the middle ground. For the more we learn about South Africa,the more it becomes apparent that the vast majority of South Africans are committed not to the authoritarian or totalitarian extremes, but to a democratic solution that provides freedom for all people. When the American public is made aware of such a commitment, the radical visions and strategies of the extremists will become less potent, and the middle ground will receive the attention it is so rightfully due.

Jill Wentzel expresses the importance of the U.S. press when she describes the damage it can cause.

> In the past, the (South African) government was sometimes like a mad dog—attacking us—but the dog was always kept on a leash. The leash was our press, organizations like the Black Sash, and, perhaps most importantly overseas press

and opinion. But there is no leash on the revolutionary Left—the American press and overseas opinion are championing their cause.[29]

Championing either extremist cause is not objective journalism, does not educate the American people and it certainly does not assist South Africa in its effort to become a nonracial, multiparty democracy. The U.S. private sector, along with the U.S. government, must recognize its limited but significant influence on South Africa. The strategies and tactics available to the U.S. private sector must be used carefully. The principal ties that connect South Africa to the United States can be found in the business community, the labor unions, the churches and the educational institutions. The objective for all these sectors should be this: resist the temptation to become a silent partner of apartheid or a romantic revolutionary supportive of violent revolutionary tactics. The authoritarian and totalitarian extremes do not deserve assistance; the democratic middle ground does. The U.S. private sector needs to promote democracy while supporting and defending those in South Africa who have rejected the racism of apartheid and the violence of the revolution.

Thirteen

Revolution or Reconciliation
What Does the Future Hold?

The situation seems to be hopeless. There are many people who begin to despair. Some leave the country. But Christians cannot afford to lose hope. Love cannot afford to lose hope.[1]

— Klaus Nurnberger

There is a moral vacuum in South Africa. The Pretoria regime, although making important steps toward reform, is a government that represents only one-fifth of the citizenry. Challenging this illegitimate authority are various revolutionary (and pseudo-revolutionary) movements, none of which can rightly claim to be the legitimate alternative government.

Although a moral vacuum exists, an absence of power does not. The Pretoria government since 1948 has ruled over a nation that has been in a state of violent, though basically stable, equilibrium. Neither the ANC nor any other revolutionary movement has been powerful enough to overthrow the government, while the government has been unable to suppress internal unrest completely. This violent equilibrium could well last until the end of the century.

What are the options that are open to those genuinely committed to South Africa's future, both in South Africa and the United States? In light of the church's tradition of a just revolution, should the leading revolutionary organization—the ANC—be supported? The five "ad bellum" criteria (borrowed from the just-war theory) constitute hurdles that must be passed before a revolution can be called "just." There is no doubt that the white minority government has caused real injury to the very people it claims to represent. In the final analysis Pretoria is a legitimate authority for less than 20 percent of the population; the vast majority have no voice in choosing their national government. But this does not mean that the ANC or any other revolutionary group automatically becomes the new "legitimate authority." The ANC is indeed a major extra-parliamentary group (albeit an armed revolutionary one) that wields a certain amount of respect and power. It does not, however, represent the legitimate authority for South Africa; there are numerous other groups (revolutionary and otherwise) equally as important and legitimate in the South Africa equation.

The ANC's ultimate intentions are somewhat unclear, but the revolutionary movement's vision for the future has not always been one that is entirely wed to democratic ideals with individual freedoms and liberties; although recently, the Congress appears to becoming more publicly committed to multi-party democracy. The threat of the oppressed simply becoming the new oppressors looms when evaluating some of the ANC's past violent revolutionary tactics.

St. Augustine cautioned that war or revolution must be initiated as a last resort. In the South African context, all peaceful channels have not been exhausted. The greatest reforms and political victories have resulted from nonviolent, usually economic, strategies and tactics. The late 1980s and early 1990s appear to be, more than ever before, offering an opportunity for radical changes without violence. Finally, the ANC's armed struggle does not have a reasonable chance of success. South Africa possesses the most sophisticated armed forces on the continent. The South African Defense Force is a highly-trained, committed military that will continue to support a white minority regime.

If armed revolution is not justified and the current regime is morally illegitimate, what are the other options? If the goal is a post-apartheid, nonracial, multi-party democracy that guarantees individual freedoms, including economic freedoms, then we in the West must support those in South Africa who are working towards these ends. We need to support the middle ground—the third

option—the democrats and liberals who have rejected the
authoritarianism of the Right and the totalitarianism of the Left. In
the late 1980s the South African middle ground is made up of
groups and individuals of all colors and backgrounds. There are
some in Parliament as well as many outside of it. They all share a
commitment to a post-apartheid nation emerging from a nonviolent, negotiated solution.

Even with its laudable ideas and strategies, the middle ground
has no guarantee of triumph in South Africa. The reactionary Right
and the revolutionary Left, in fact, are often better organized and
appear more likely to succeed. The dice are undoubtedly loaded in
their favor. (This is not to suggest that there is going to be a
decisive "victor" in the near future. In fact, the state of violent
equilibrium will most likely continue.)

History has not always been kind to the middle ground; the
democrats of South Africa have a daunting and dangerous task
ahead of them. The tragic fate of the middle ground in Algeria in
the 1950s is not lost upon those in South Africa today. The objective of Ben Bella and the revolutionary movement was not to defeat
the French army—that was beyond its capacity. Rather, their
strategy was aimed directly at eliminating moderates, those attempting to build a multi-racial society, whether they were French
or Arab. Ben Bella's written orders were:

> Liquidate all personalities who want to play the role of
> interlocutor. Kill any person attempting to deflect the
> militants, kill all those who pay taxes and those who collect
> them.[2]

The only way for the moderates in Algeria to survive was either
by joining the extremes or leaving the country.

The middle ground in South Africa must resist with every
moral and prudent means available the polarization sweeping the
country. To be forced into abandoning their nation or joining the
extremes is no choice. Unfortunately, that pattern is already beginning to emerge. Many whites, and the few blacks who have the
resources, are emigrating. South Africans, either out of despera-
tion, coercion or some romantic naiveté have signed up with the
armed revolution or have thrown in with the neo-fascist Right. The
ranks of the middle ground appear to be slowly shrinking.

Those who represent forces for moderation in South Africa,

bolstered by like-minded democrats in the U.S., must go on the offensive. Some already have, and very tangible results such as the Kwa-Natal Indaba and the Soweto rent negotiations which have resulted from their endeavors. The middle ground's approach must include not only resisting polarization fed by the extremes, but also attempting to reverse that extreme divisiveness and broaden its own base of support. That is, the moderate democrats must tap the extremes for support. When the Pretoria regime speaks and acts as if it is serious about radical reform, the democrats must applaud and encourage it. Likewise, when the ANC talks of multi-party democracies and free or mixed economic structures, the middle ground needs to reinforce it. These potential encouraging signs from the Left and Right must be assessed with a realistic political eye. There is a large risk of being co-opted by either extreme, and when that happens the victory will belong to the extremes.

The emergence of a truly democratic, nonracial South Africa would be equivalent to the birth of a new nation. It is to be hoped that the emphasis will fall less on who governs and more on how the nation will be governed. Oscar Dhlomo often asks, "How many more golden opportunities for interracial harmony and cooperation in this country are we going to miss?"[3] Unfortunately, the answer is probably as many as it takes before all sides recognize that negotiations are the only positive path open. The middle ground's job is to hold the center together, maintaining its democratic ideals and values until that day arrives. It is also the task of the democrats in South Africa and the United States to push and cajole and pray and sweat to make that day come sooner rather than later.

The middle ground's task is enormous, but there are tools currently available to achieve the goals. The economy remains a vital instrument in eroding apartheid and resisting armed revolution. As the black community continues to increase its economic power, its political leverage will increase. Negotiations, primarily on second-tier and municipal levels, have recently offered a bright ray of hope. The church community, although as fractured as the society at large, is faithfully attempting to pursue reconciliation. All of these factors work toward the development and success of the democratic element within South Africa, and all of them need to be assisted by American democrats with a common vision. As one South African sadly wrote,

What we have in South Africa is the setting for a Greek

tragedy. The actors may each oppose apartheid. But all are caught inescapably in webs of their own little worlds and prejudices. They can't do anything about it. As with all tragedies, you know it must end in disaster.[4]

Disaster for South Africa is the easy way out. Joining or encouraging an armed revolution is deceptively simple. So too is acquiescing to apartheid. The hard challenges, the tough tasks, are for those who have enough faith and hope and patience and optimism that South Africa's future is not the future of a tragedy, but rather the future of a bright, prosperous and free nation.

Notes

Chapter One

1. See J.F. Childress and J. Macquarrie, editors, *Dictionary of Christian Ethics* (Philadelphia: Westminster Press, 1986), 446.

2. See George Weigel, *Tranquillitas Ordinis: The Present Failure and Future Promise of American Catholic Thought on War and Peace* (New York: Oxford University Press, 1987).

3. Leo Tolstoy, "What I Believe," *The Tolstoy Centenary Collection* (London: 1928).

4. See Weigel, *Tranquillitas Ordinis*, 246.

5. *Ibid.*, 278.

6. See J.T. Johnson, "Crusade," in *Dictionary of Christian Ethics*, 139.

7. Quoted in *Tranquillitas Ordinis*, 39.

8. Paul Johnson, *A History of Christianity* (Harmondsworth: Penguin Books, 1978), 244.

9. Quoted in Weigel, *Tranquillitas Ordinis*, 39.

10. For excellent abbreviated discussions, see James Turner Johnson's "Just War," in J. Macquarrie, editor, *Christian Ethics* (Philadelphia: Westminster Press, 1986) or George Weigel, *Peace and Freedom*, (Washington, D.C.: Institute on Religion and Democracy, 1983).

11. Quoted in Weigel, *Peace and Freedom*, 13.

12. St. Thomas Aquinas, *Summa Theologiae*, from the Black Friars' edition, (New York: McGraw-Hill, 1972), 80-85.

13. Aquinas, *Summa Theologiae*, 80.

14. *Ibid.*, 80.

15. See Weigel, *Tranquillitas Ordinis*.

16. J. Macquarrie, *The Concept of Peace* (New York: Harper and Row, 1973), 57.

17. *Ibid.*,

18. Aquinas, *Summa Theologiae*, 80.

19. Macquarrie, *The Concept of Peace*, 56.

20. *Ibid.*, 56.

21. *Ibid.*, 58.

22. See John Gunnemann, "Revolution," in John Macquarrie, *Christian Ethics*.

23. Macquarrie, *The Concept of Peace*, 57.

24. Richard John Neuhaus and Peter Berger, *Movement and Revolution* (New York: Anchor Books, 1970).

25. Aquinas, *Summa Theologiae*, 85.

26. A. Holmes, *War and Christian Ethics* (Grand Rapids, Michigan: 1975), 17.

27. *Complete Works of Lenin*, vol. 38, 337.

28. C. West, *Ethics, Violence and Revolution* (New York: 1969), 60.

29. Neuhaus and Berger, *Movement and Revolution*, 191.

30. William Raspberry, "South Africa: Land of No Compromise," *Washington Post* (February 1987).

31. Quoted in Richard John Neuhaus, *Dispensations* (Grand Rapids: Eerdmans, 1986), 266.

Chapter Two

1. St. Thomas Aquinas, as quoted in Weigel, *Tranquillitas Ordinas*, 36.

2. Neuhaus and Berger, *Movement and Revolution*, 189.

3. Archbishop Desmond Tutu, speech to foreign correspondents, Cape Town, March 17, 1987.

4. South African government figures as released to the *New York Times* (February 13, 1987).

5. Conversation with Mr. Joe Seremane, Director Justice & Reconciliation Division, South African Council of Churches, Johannesburg, May 16, 1989.

6. *The Economist* (September 27, 1986) and *Business Day* (Johannesburg, October 6, 1986).

Chapter Three

1. Quoted in Neuhaus, *Dispensations*.

2. See A. Freudenschuss, "Legal and Political Aspects of the Recognition of National Liberation Movements" in *Millennium: Journal of International Studies*, volume II, no. 2, 116.

3. Oliver Tambo, address at the 75th Anniversary of the ANC (Lusaka, Zambia, January 8, 1987).

4. *Ibid.*

5. "An Interview with Oliver Tambo," *Nightline*, ABC News, New York, January 28, 1987.

6. Oliver Tambo, address at the 25th Anniversary of the Umkhonto we Sizwe (Lusaka, Zambia, December 16, 1986).

7. Department of State Report to Congress, *Communist Influence in South Africa*, January 1987. The report was produced in fulfillment of Section 509 of the Anti-Apartheid Act of 1986.

8. Thomas Karis, "South African Liberation: The Communist Factor," *Foreign Affairs* (winter 1986/87), 271.

9. *Ibid.*

10. Conversation with Ken Owen, Johannesburg, March 12, 1987.

11. Department of State Report to Congress, "Communist Influence in South Africa."

12. Mike Calabrese and Mike Kendall, "The Black Agenda for South Africa," *The Nation* (October 26, 1985).

13. Conversation with Archbishop Denis Hurley, Durban, March 23, 1987.

14. "Union Chief Vows to End Apartheid," *Washington Post* (July 16, 1987).

15. "Black South African, in U.S. Exile, Works to Help Unions Back Home," *Christian Science Monitor* (November 10, 1986), 7.

16. Karis, "South African Liberation," 269-70.

17. *Ibid.*, 270.

18. Elijah Barayi (President of COSATU), *South Africa International* (April 1987), 17.

19. Alfred Nzo, address at the 65th Anniversary of the South African Communist Party (London, July 30, 1986).

20. Quoted in *Leadership*, vol. 5 (1986). See also *Clarion Call*, vol. 2 (Inkatha, 1986).

21. *A U.S. Policy Toward South Africa*, Report of the Secretary of State's Advisory Committee on South Africa (Washington D.C., January 1987).

22. "Civil Wars, Frontline Comment," *Frontline* (Johannesburg: February 1987), 4.

23. As quoted in *Ecumenical Press* Service (World Council of Churches, Geneva, Switzerland) 87.05.65.

24. Gatsha Buthelezi, "The Plight of Responsible Black Leaders in South Africa," speech at Boston University, November 17, 1986.

25. "Buthelezi Quotes ANC Call For Violence," (Johannesburg, SABA Wire Service, October 2, 1985).

26. Quoted in Neuhaus, *Dispensations*, 272.

27. *Ibid.*

28. "We Are Fighting for the Seizure of Power," ANC Radio Freedom commentary, Addis Ababa (in English to South Africa), December 19, 1985 (EA201347).

29. John de St. Jorre, "South Africa Embattled," *Foreign Affairs 65*, no. 3.

30. Conversation with Tom Lodge, Johannesburg, March 16, 1987.

31. "South Africa: The Opposition Phalanx," *Africa Confidential* (December 11, 1985).

32. Quoted in *Washington Times* (January 29, 1987).

33. Mark Uhlig, "Inside the ANC," *New York Times Magazine* (October 12, 1986).

34. Conversation with Frank Martin, Durban, March 23, 1987.

35. Karis, "South African Liberation," 284; Gustov Spohn, "Reports of Civilian Attacks by WCC—Supported Anti-Apartheid Group," *Religious News Service*, November 29, 1988, 1.

36. Joe Slovo, address at the Second MPLA-Labor Party Congress, Luanda, Angola, December 10, 1985.

37. Quoted in *Independent* (London, November 10, 1986).

38. Steven Mufson, "The War for South Africa," *Washington Post* (December 14, 1986), 1 (Outlook section).

39. Resolution of the United Nations General Assembly (1974), No.3411 G (XXX).

40. "Revolutionary Warfare: "Legitimacy and Recognition," ISSUP *Strategic Review* (December 1984).

41. Peter Walshe, "The ANC—Part of the Solution in South Africa," *Christianity and Crisis* (May 4, 1987), 164.

42. Tambo, address at the ANC 65th Anniversary.

43. *Ibid.*

44. Alfred Nzo, address at the 65th Anniversary of the South African Communist Party (London, July 30, 1986).

45. *Ibid.*

46. Conversation with Tom Lodge, Johannesburg, March 16, 1987.

47. *Ibid.*

48. Quoted in *Sunday Times* (March 11, 1986).

49. Conversation with Solly Smith, London, March 9, 1987.

50. Nomavenda Mathiane, "The Deadly Duel of the Warares and the Zim-Zims," *Frontline* (February 1987).

51. "Civil Wars, Frontline Comment," *Frontline* (February 1987).

52. Cited in "Tensions Mount Between Factions of Anti-Apartheid," *Washington Times* (December 5, 1986).

53. Mathiane, "The Deadly Duel."

54. Quoted in *New York Times Review of Books* (February 12, 1987).

55. Quoted in *New York Times Magazine* (October 12, 1986), 20.

56. Archbishop Desmond Tutu, speech at his enthronement as Bishop of Johannesburg.

57. Conversation with Archbishop Denis Hurley, Durban, March 23, 1987.

58. John Chettle, testimony before the U.S. Secretary of State's Advisory Committee on South Africa, July 1986.

59. Mathiane, "The Deadly Duel."

60. Conversation with a South African worker, Durban, March 1987.

61. Conversation with Ken Owen, Johannesburg, March 16, 1987.

62. Patrick Lawrence, "Do ANC Leaders Have Control?" *Christian Science Monitor* (July 11, 1986).

63. Conversation with Tom Lodge, Johannesburg, March 16, 1987.

64. Quoted in "Pretoria Faces Tough Odds in New Effort to Win Over Urban Blacks," *Christian Science Monitor* (April 9, 1987), 1.

65. Conversation with Archbishop Denis Hurley.

66. Quoted in "The Black Agenda for South Africa," *The Nation* (October 26, 1985).

67. *A U.S. Policy For South Africa*, Report of the Secretary of State's Advisory Committee on South Africa.

68. "An Editor's Report on Attitudes in South Africa," *Public Opinion* (Sept.-Oct. 1986), 55.

69. Paul Malherbe, "South Africa: What About the Democratic Option," *Washington Post* (January 27, 1987), A19.

70. Conversation with Craig Williamson, Sandton S.A., March

24, 1987. Williamson is a former ANC official and informer for the South African security police.
    71. Conversation with Gavin Maasdrop, Durban, March 20, 1987.
    72. Tambo, address at the Unkhonto we Sizwe 25th Anniversary.

Chapter Four

1. Michael Walzer, *Just and Unjust Wars* (New York: Basic Books, 1977).
    2. Neuhaus and Berger, *Movement and Revolution*, 204.
    3. "Dumi Matabani on South Africa," interview, National Public Radio (Washington D.C., August 7, 1986).
    4. *Ibid.*
    5. *Colonialism of a Special Type*, ANC, London, 3.
    6. Freedom Charter, ANC.
    7. *Colonialism of a Special Type*, 3.
    8. *Communist Influence in South Africa*, State Department Report to Congress, (January 1987).
    9. Rusty Bernstein and Michael Harmel's names were suggested as authors of the Freedom Charter by Mr. R. J. Arenstein, himself a former member of the SAC
    10. Quoted in *The Guardian* (London, August 17, 1986).
    11. Conversation with Tom Lodge, Johannesburg, March 16, 1987.
    12. *Ibid.*
    13. *Ibid.*
    14. "Dumi Matabani," National Public Radio.
    15. Mark Uhlig, "Inside the ANC."
    16. "We Are Fighting For Power," commentary, ANC Radio Freedom, Addis Ababa, December 24, 1985.
    17. *Ibid.*
    18. Commentary, ANC Radio Freedom, Addis Ababa, May 7, 1986.
    19. *Ibid.*
    20. "Tambo Says Violence Inevitable," *Washington Post* (January 27, 1987).
    21. Tambo, address at Umkhonto we Sizwe 25th Anniversary, December 16, 1986.

22. Quoted in *Liberalism and the Middle Ground* (South African Institute on Race Relations, 1986) 42.

23. Quoted in Neuhaus, *Dispensations*, 287.

24. *African Communist* (No. 87, Fourth quarter 1981).

25. Joe Slovo, address at the 65th Anniversary of the SACP (London, July 30, 1986).

26. For a comprehensive examination of Marxist analysis in South Africa, see Butler, Elphik & Welsh, *Democratic Liberalism in South Africa* (Middleton, CT: Wesleyan University Press, 1987).

27. Quoted in Karis, "South African Liberation."

28. *African Communist* (No. 92, October 1, 1983), 81-82.

29. Joe Slovo, address at SACP 65th Anniversary.

30. See *The Economist* (July 26, 1986).

31. Bartholomew Hlapane, testimony before the Subcommittee on Security and Terrorism to the Committee on the Judiciary, United States Senate, November 1982.

32. See *Washington Times* (April 22, 1987).

33. Conversation with Tom Lodge.

34. "Soviets in Shift, Press for Accord in South Africa," *New York Times*, March 1989, A1.

35. As quoted in *Background Brief*, Foreign and Commnwealth Office, London, February 1989, 6.

36. *New York Times*, March 16, 1989, A1.

37. *Ibid.*

38. "A 1988 Update on Soviet Relations with Pretoria, the ANC and the SACP," *CSIS Africa Notes*, September 1, 1988, Washington, D.C., 4.

39. *New York Times*, March 16, 1989, A1.

40. G. Starushenko, "Conference of Peace, Cooperation and Social Progress," *Financial Times* (London, January 25, 1987) and *Johannesburg Star* (January 25, 1987).

41. Dr. R. Nel, "For Moscow the Waiting Game Pays," *Ehergos 14* (1986), 42.

42. *Ibid*, 53.

43. *Ibid*, 53.

44. *Ibid*, 51.

45. Tambo, address at ANC 75th Anniversary.

46. Joe Slovo, address at Conway Hall in London during 65th Anniversary of SACP (July 1986) and reported in *Manchester Guardian* (August 4, 1986).

47. *Ibid.*

48. *NUSAS Talks to the ANC* (Harare, Zimbabwe; National Union of South African Students, March 31-April 2, 1985).

49. *Colonialism of a Special Type*, 3.

50. "Dumi Matabane," National Public Radio.

51. Conversation with Solly Smith, London, March 7, 1987.

52. Conversation with Tom Lodge.

53. *Ibid.*

54. Quoted in *Leadership* (Capetown: January 1986).

55. "The Lusaka Amendments," Tom Lodge, *Leadership*, Vol. 7, No. 4, 1988, 17.

56. *Ibid*, 19.

57. *Ibid*, 19.

58. ANC Radio Freedom, May 4, 1986.

59. "General Coetzee's Report on Terrorism," *Weekly Mail* (May 23-29, 1986).

60. Quoted in *New York Times Magazine* (May 10, 1986), 44.

61. *Ibid.*

62. Alfred Nzo, *London Sunday Times* and *The Daily News* (September 16, 1986).

63. Conversation with Solly Smith.

64. *Ibid.*

Chapter Five

1. C. West, *Ethics, Violence and Revolution*, 60.

2. Conversation with Rev. Robert Robertson, Johannesburg, March 11, 1987.

3. Conversation with Ken Owen, Johannesburg, March 16, 1987.

4. *Washington Post*, December 2, 1986, A26 and *South Africa Foundation News* (Johannesburg, January 1987).

5. Quoted in "Suzman Looks Ahead," *Inside South Africa (February 1987)*.

6. Conversation with Dr. 0. Dhlomo, Durban, March 21, 1987.

7. Ken Owen, "Liberalism: What Kind of South Africa?" in

Liberalism and the Middle Ground (Johannesburg: South Africa Institute on Race Relations: 1986).

8. See S. Sethi, "Economic Leverage," Baruch College, City University of New York.

9. Conversation with Sheena Duncan, Johannesburg, March 16, 1987.

10. Buthelezi, *The East-West Papers* (October 1986).

11. Conversation with John Kane-Berman, Johannesburg, March 10, 1987.

12. Quoted in *Time* (May 4, 1987).

13. NGK (Dutch Reformed Church) General Synod, October 1986, paragraph 320.

14. Quoted in *Inside South Africa* (March 1987), 6.

15. Conversation with W. Esterhuyse, Stellenbosch, March 19, 1987.

16. "Revolt at Stellenbosch Strikes at Heart of Apartheid," *Wall Street Journal* (March 6, 1987).

17. W. Esterhuyse, *Sunday Times* (Johannesburg: March 15, 1987).

18. See Ken Owen, "Liberalism: What Kind of South Africa?"

19. See *Time* (May 4, 1987).

20. *Ibid.*

21. Conversation with C. Mouton, Durban, March 24, 1987.

22. Speech by State President W. Botha, September 30, 1985.

23. W. Botha, Speech Opening Parliament, January 31, 1986.

24. Quoted in *Inside South Africa* (April 1987), 67.

25. *Los Angeles Times* (October 2, 1986).

26. Quoted in *Washington Post* (June 12, 1987).

27. "De Klerk Speech Spells Out 'Justice for All' Vision," *Business Day*, Johannesburg, May 15, 1989.

28. Inkatha, *Clarion Call*, 3 (1986).

29. Quoted in *Wall Street Journal* (May 6, 1987).

Chapter Six

1. Neuhaus and Berger, *Movement and Revolution*, 259.

2. Conversation with Tom Lodge, Johannesburg, March 16, 1987.

3. Oliver Tambo, address at the 75th anniversary of the ANC.

4. "Rebel Plans More Violence," *Washington Post* (February 1, 1985).

5. "Dumi Matabane," National Public Radio. When asked how the ANC would "dig out the Afrikaners," Matabane responded, "Perhaps the U.S. will give us arms."

6. *A Policy Toward South Africa*, Report of the Secretary of State's Advisory Committee on South Africa, 21.

7. Conversation with South African Embassy spokesman, Washington D.C., June 22, 1987.

8. See St. Jorre, "South Africa Embattled," *Foreign Affairs*.

9. Conversation with former SADF officer, Pretoria, March 20, 1987.

10. Quoted in *Washington Post* (February 10, 1987), A18.

11. Quoted in Neuhaus, *Dispensations*, 248.

12. Inkatha, *Clarion Call 1* (1986).

13. Derrick Thema, "A Vision Which Could Save South Africa," *Inside South Africa* (June 1987).

14. Conversation with Frank Martin, Durban, March 19, 1987.

15. Conversation with Archbishop Denis Hurley.

16. Robert Taylor, *The War of the Flea*, (London: Lutterworth Press, 1982), 43.

17. Conversation with Ken Owen.

18. Conversation with Tom Lodge.

19. Quoted in *Washington Post* (November 25, 1986), E2.

Chapter Seven

1. John Macquarrie, *The Concept of Peace*, as quoted in George Weigel, *Peace & Freedom* (Washington D.C.: Institute on Religion and Democracy, 1983).

2. See Kairos Document discussion in Chapter 10.

Chapter Eight

1. Quoted in *Washington Post* (November 25, 1986), E2.

2. "Liberalism—Past and Present: An Interview with Ernest Wentzel," *Frontline* (June 1985).

3. Conversation with Chris Saunders, Durban, March 24, 1987.

4. Ken Owen, "Liberalism: What Kind of South Africa," *Liberalism and the Middle Ground*.

Chapter Nine

1. Conversation with Sheena Duncan.
2. Jill Wentzel, letter to a South African colleague, Johannesburg, November 18, 1985.
3. *Ibid.*
4. *Ibid.*
5. Jill Wentzel, "The Liberal Slide-Away," *Liberation and the Middle Ground*, (Johannesburg: Institute on Race Relations, 1986).
6. Jill Wentzel, letter to a South African colleague.
7. Ken Owen, *Sunday Times* (March 2, 1986).
8. Jill Wentzel, letter to a South African colleague.
9. Conversation with W. Esterhuyse.
10. Ken Owen, *Sunday Times* (March 2, 1986).
11. Aggrey Klaaste as quoted by Peter Younghusband, "Internal Power Plays Devastate Black South Africans," *Washington Times* (November 2, 1987).

Chapter Ten

1. Desmond Tutu, "The Process of Reconciliation and the Demand of Obedience," *Transformation* (April/June 1986) 3, no. 2, 7.
2. John Kane-Berman, "Attacking Apartheid's Underbelly," *Leadership 6*, no. 1 (1987).
3. *Ibid.*
4. *Ibid.*
5. "Suzman Looks Ahead," *Inside South Africa* (Cape Town: February 1987).
6. Conversation with Dr. Gavin Maasdorp, Durban, March 23, 1987.
7. Conversation with Maasdorp and *Washington Times* (March 30, 1987).
8. *Weekly Mail* (Johannesburg, July 25-31, 1986), 4.
9. Report of the U.S. Secretary of State's Advisory Committee on South Africa, 6.
10. Ambassador Alan Keyes' testimony before the House Subcommittee on African Affairs (June 16, 1987).
11. Foundation for Africa's Future briefing report on the "Anti-Apartheid Act of 1986" (October 30,1987).

12. "Into the Black," *The Economist,* London, November 5, 1988.

13. *Ibid.*

14. South African Catholic Bishop's Conference, "Report on Economic Pressure" (Durban, March 1987).

15. Abraham Lincoln, First Inaugural Address, Washington D.C., 1861.

16. Report of the Secretary of State's Advisory Committee on South Africa.

17. Dr. Pierre du Toit, *South Africa International* (Johannesburg: July 1986).

18. The Report of the Secretary of State's Advisory Committee on South Africa, 20.

19. "An Editor's Report on Attitudes in South Africa," *Public Opinion* (Sept.-Oct. 1986), 55.

20. Desmond Clarence, "Indaba," *Leadership* (Cape Town: 1987), vol. 6, 1.

21. Conversation with Peter Mansfield, Durban, March 20, 1987.

22. Conversation with Chris Saunders, Durban, March 23, 1987.

23. Conversation with Peter Mansfield.

24. Conversation with a cabinet minister, Somerset West, March 19, 1987.

25. Conversation with John Kane-Berman, Johannesburg, March 10, 1987.

26. Conversation with Oscar Dhlomo (Secretary-General, Inkatha), Durban, March 21, 1987.

27. A broad coalition was formed in early 1987 in the Transvaal to examine the Indaba process. Initially known as the "Alliance for Realists," it includes representatives from the PFP, Labour Party, United Municipalities of South Africa, Solidarity and others.

28. For an interview with the authors of *South Africa: The Solution* (Amagi Publishing: 1986); see "South Africa: Is There a Solution?" Briefing Paper No. 8 (Institute on Religion and Democracy: March 1987).

29. Poll by Markinor, Inc. cited in *Washington Post* (May 18, 1987).

30. Conversation with Sheena Duncan, Johannesburg, March 16, 1987).

31. Quoted in *Washington Post* (June 12, 1987).

32. Quoted in *Manchester Guardian* (U.K., June 26, 1987).

33. See "South Africa Blacks' New Tactic Fazes Pretoria," *Christian Science Monitor,* January 26, 1989 and "Major New Initiative on Soweto," *Business Day,* March 17, 1989.

34. *Ibid.*

35. Governor Phatudi, speech for "Alliance for Realists," Pretoria, March 14, 1987.

36. Conversation with Michael Cassidy, Pietermaritzburg, March 25, 1987.

37. See Oliver O'Donovan's "Reconciliation," *The Westminster Dictionary of Christian Ethics* (Philadelphia: Westminster, 1986), 528.

38. The Report of the Secretary of State's Advisory Committee on South Africa.

39. See The Report of the Secretary of State's Advisory Committee on South Africa; and "Can the Church Mend the Anguish of a Nation?" *Christianity Today Institute* (November 21, 1986).

40. Nico Smith, "Christian Fellowship Helps Break Barriers," *Religious News Service* (September 16, 1986).

41. For instance, Bishop Michael Nuttal, Anglican Bishop of Natal, has initiated special reconciliation courses for his diocesan leaders.

42. Conversation with W. Esterhuyse, Stellenbosch, March 11, 1987.

43. Conversation with Michael Nuttal, Natal, March 20, 1987.

44. Conversation with Ken Owen, Johannesburg, March 16, 1987.

45. *The Kairos Document: A Theological Comment on the Political Crisis in South Africa* (September 1985). For an excellent brief analysis of the Kairos Document see *Religion and Democracy* (Institute on Religion and Democracy, July/August 1986).

46. *Ibid.*

47. *Ibid.*

48. *Ibid.*

49. *Ibid.*

50. *Ibid.*

51. *Ibid.*

52. *Ibid.*

53. Quoted in *The Guardian* (London, March 25, 1987).

54. Quoted in "Key Church Splits in South Africa," *Washington Post (June 28, 1987)*.

55. Alan Boesak, Religion and Society Lecture Series, Messiah College, Grantham, Pennsylvania, March 5, 1987.

56. Boesak, Religion and Society Lecture Series.

57. Quoted in "Can the Church Mend the Anguish of a Nation?" *Christianity Today Institute (November 21, 1986)*.

58. Reinhold Niebuhr, *The Children of Light and the Children of Darkness* (New York: Scribner, 1944), xiii.

59. See Jacques Barzun, *Is Democratic Theory for Export?* (New York: Carnegie Council on Ethics and International Affairs, 1986).

60. Conversation with Sheena Duncan, Johannesburg, March 16, 1987.

61. Klaus Nurnberger, *Conflict Resolution in South Africa: An Exercise in Political Ethics,* (Pretoria: Institute on Race Relations, 1986).

62. Conversation with Klaus Nurnberger (professor of theology, University of South Africa), Pietermaritzburg, March 25, 1987.

Chapter Eleven

1. Bobby Godsell, "South Africa After the Elections," Briefing Luncheon, Institute on Religion and Democracy, New York, June 1987.

2. Report of The Secretary of State's Advisory Committee on South Africa.

3. Helen Kitchen and Michael Clough, *The U.S. and South Africa: Realities and Red Herrings,* (Washington, D.C.: Center for Strategic and International Studies, 1984).

4. Bobby Godsell and Peter Berger, "Fantasies About South Africa," *Commentary*, July 1987.

5. Senator Edward Kennedy, testimony before the Senate Banking, Housing and Urban Affairs Committee, Washington D.C., June 1986.

6. The "Alternative Recommendations" of the Committee's Report were written by John Dellenback, Lawrence Eagleburger and Roger Smith.

7. See "U.S. Churches Betray Moderates," *Seattle Times* (July 21, 1987).

8. Paul Freedenburg, testimony before the House sub-committee on African Affairs, June 16, 1987.

9. "Self-Inflicted Sanctions," *Wall Street Journal*, May 5, 1988.

10. *Ibid.*, and Foundation for Africa's Foundation, *Report*, May 5, 1988.

11. Foundation for Africa's Future.

12. *Communist Influence in South Africa*, State Department Report to Congress.

13. Conversation with Tom Lodge, Johannesburg, March 16, 1987.

14. Conversation with Bishop M. Nuttal, Durban, March 20, 1987.

15. Conversation with Dr. Oscar Dhlomo, Durban, March 21, 1987.

Chapter Twelve

1. Conversation with Nana Mahoma, Washington D.C., February 10, 1987.

2. Reverend M. Lorenzo Shepard at the Churches' Emergency Committee on Southern Africa (CECSA), Washington, D.C., January 1986.

3. Report of The U.S. Secretary of State's Advisory Committee on South Africa.

4. W. Ebersohn, "The Conscientious Investors," *Leadership*, vol. 7, 1988.

5. Quoted in *Religious News Service* (June 3, 1987).

6. Sal G. Marzullo, *America*, August 3-10, 1986, vol. 153, no. 3, 53.

7. Leon Sullivan, press conference (Washington D.C., December 1980). See *Church Economic Programs Information Service (CEPIS Bulletin)*, (Washington, DC: IRD, January 1987).

8. Conversation with Rudolph Agnew, London, March 6, 1987.

9. *Inside South Africa* (June 1987), 17.

10. Sam Motsuenvane, "Nafcoc in Search of Solutions in Southern Africa," *South Africa International* (October 1986).

11. Quoted in "South African Unions Take Anti-Apartheid Lead," *Wall Street Journal* (July 22, 1987).

12. Quoted in "Union Chief Vows to End Apartheid," *Washington Post* (July 16, 1987).

13. Quoted in "South African Unions Take Anti-Apartheid Lead."

14. *Ibid.*

15. *Harare Declaration,* adopted in Harare, Zimbabwe, December 16, 1985.

16. *United Methodist News Service,* December 10, 1985.

17. *Ibid.*

18. Churches' Emergency Committee on Southern Africa meeting, Washington D.C., January 1986.

19. Churches' Emergency Committee on Southern Africa meeting, Washington D.C., June 16, 1986.

20. CECSA spokesperson, telephone interview with *CEPIS Bulletin,* June 15, 1986.

21. *Religious News Service,* July 23, 1986.

22. The Right Reverend John Walker, testimony before the Senate Foreign Relations Committee, July 24, 1986.

23. *Ibid.*

24. Letter to "100 Top Corporations in South Africa," CECSA, August 22, 1986.

25. *Weekly News Wrap-Up* (May 22, 1987), 4.

26. Johan Heyns, remarks at Institute on Religion and Democracy luncheon, Washington D.C., June 10, 1987.

27. Report of The Secretary of State's Advisory Committee on South Africa.

28. Conversation with Gavin Maasdorp, Durban, March 24, 1987.

29. Conversation with Jill Wentzel, Johannesburg, March 12, 1987.

Chapter Thirteen

1. Klaus Nurnberger, "Costly Reconciliation," *Conflict Resolution in South Africa* (Pretoria: June 19, 1986).

2. Paul Johnson's analysis of the FCA in Algeria, as quoted in *Liberalism and the Middle Ground* (Institute on Race Relations, 1986).

3. Conversation with Oscar Dhlomo, Durban, March 21, 1987.
4. Quoted in "Can the Church Mend the Anguish of a Nation?" *Christianity Today Institute* (November 21, 1986).

Glossary

ad bellum criteria. Within Christian tradition there are five criteria that must be fulfilled before a war can be considered "just."

ANC. African National Congress, formed in 1912 and banned since 1960. It is still the leading advocate for an armed revolution in South Africa. Currently, its international headquarters is in Lusaka, Zambia.

AWB. Afrikaner Resistance Movement was formed in the early 1980s as a political and paramilitary organization that is committed to the apartheid structure. It has pledged its political and military clout in resisting any forms of "power-sharing."

AZAPO. Azanian People's Organization. Formed in 1978 by black intellectuals, AZAPO has its roots within the PAC and the black consciousness movement.

Broederbond. A "brotherhood," or cultural organization whose primary purpose is to sustain and preserve Afrikaner culture. The Broederbond has become an important breeding ground for Afrikaner leaders.

Churches' Emergency Committee on Southern Africa (CECSA). Formed in 1986 by a group of U.S. mainline churches, the Committee was a leading force in the fight for economic sanctions against South Africa.

COSATU. Confederation of South African Trade Unions, formed in 1985, is South Africa's largest trade union federation with more than 600,000 members.

Comprehensive Anti-Apartheid Act. Passed by the U.S. Congress in 1986, the CAAA established a variety of economic sanctions against South Africa.

CP. The Conservative Party in 1987 emerged as the National Party's official opposition in Parliament. To the Right of the NP, the CP calls for an adherence to the apartheid structure and "power-sharing" that follows a policy of segregation.

Democratic Enhancement. A policy for the U.S. public and private sector to implement in its efforts to eliminate apartheid while laying the foundation for a democratic South Africa. This strategy focuses on supporting the "democratic middle ground" in South Africa.

Freedom Charter. First drafted in 1955, it is the ANC's published document that expresses its visions and aspirations.

FRELIMO. This is the official party of the government of Mozambique.

Front-line states. The black independent nations that are South Africa's neighbors. They include Angola, Zimbabwe, Botswana, Mozambique, Zambia and Tanzania.

Group Areas Act. Officially still on the books, this apartheid law designates South African residential areas as "white" or "black." Since the early 1980s, "gray" or mixed areas have begun to emerge.

Indaba. An Indaba or "high council" was convened in March 1986 by the Natal Provincial Council and the KwaZulu government. The Indaba drafted a constitutional framework for a newly created "KwaNatal" government that would extend the same voting rights to all people within Natal and KwaZulu. The Indaba's "second tier" or provincial proposals have yet to be approved by the central government.

Inkatha. Traditionally a Zulu cultural organization; Chief Buthelezi revived the group in 1974 and transformed it into South Africa's largest legal black political organization. It has more than one million members, primarily Zulus.

Kairos Document. In 1985 a number of South African theologians published *The Kairos Document : A Theological Comment on the Political Crisis in South Africa.* The document endorses "prophetic theology" and makes use of a "social analysis" which is firmly rooted in class conflict.

Mixed-Marriages Act. One of apartheid's primary social laws which prohibited marriage across racial lines. It was abolished in 1985.

MPLA. The official party for the Marxist-oriented government of Angola.

NACTU. National Council of Trade Unions, South Africa's second largest labor union confederation has more than 300,000 members.

NGK. The Dutch Reformed Church, frequently referred to as the "National Party at prayer, " is the largest white church in South Africa.

NP. The National Party has been in control of the South

African government since 1948. It holds a large majority of the seats in Parliament.

PAC. Pan Africanist Congress was formed in 1959 as a break away group from the ANC. PAC leaders left the ANC out of a commitment to "black consciousness"; they perceived the ANC as straying from its African nationalist goals. PAC, outlawed in South Africa, is headquartered in Dar es Salaam, Tanzania.

Pass Laws. Officially known as Influx Control laws, this primary pillar of apartheid regulated where non-whites could live and work and travel in South Africa. They were phased out in the early 1980s.

The People's War. The ANC has been committed to armed revolution since 1961, and the concept of a "people's war" has become the rhetorical banner for extending the revolution into every part of South African society.

PFP. The Progressive Federal Party was the official opposition party (to the National Party) in South Africa's Parliament until 1987. The PFP, more liberal than the NP, is now the third largest white political party after the NP and CP.

SACP. South African Communist Party is a small outlawed organization. Its importance rests with its alliance with the ANC.

State of Emergency. Imposed in June 1986, the State of Emergency allows for extended detentions without charges and greatly limits certain civil rights.

UDF. The United Democratic Front is an umbrella organization that represents a coalition of 600-700 groups that include political, community, labor, religious and youth organizations. The UDF has endorsed the Freedom Charter and echoes some of the ANC's goals and aspirations.

Umkonto we Sizwe (MK). "Spear of the Nation" is the African National Congress's military wing.

Index